Terra

What people are saying about …

SHRINKING THE INTEGRITY GAP

"Great leaders are characterized by virtues such as courage, vision, and decisiveness. But there's one quality that should be at the top of every leader's priority list: integrity. This book offers a vital and timeless message for those who desire to be above reproach in their leadership."

Jim Daly, president, Focus on the Family

"Ever since we have known Jeff and Terra, they have had a passion to help leaders. Being an emotionally healthy leader is extremely challenging, and the Mattsons will help you identify the biggest obstacles for becoming a wholehearted leader."

Tristen Collins, LPC, and Jonathan Collins, cofounder of The Bible Project and coauthors of *Why Emotions Matter*

"We're long overdue for a trauma-informed, evidence-based, practical, and biblical guide to wholehearted and integrous leadership. Jeff and Terra Mattson have written just that book and are the real deal. This powerhouse couple are wrapping their arms around leaders everywhere who need personal mentors to coach them out of denial to healing and Wholehearted Leadership."

Michelle Watson, PhD, LPC, author of *Let's Talk* and radio/podcast host of *The Dad Whisperer*

"We've known Jeff and Terra for a long time and can attest to the fact that they are a living example of this powerful book. Whether you are a leader who is just getting started or you're a seasoned veteran, you won't want to miss out on their message."

Drs. Les & Leslie Parrott, #1 *New York Times*
bestselling authors of *Healthy Me, Healthy Us*

"Jeff and Terra Mattson are seasoned counselors who've journeyed through real-life scenarios with many pastors and other ministry leaders. Not only are they expert voices but they embody the values their book offers. You can trust these messengers. I do because they live what they preach."

Randy Remington, president,
US Foursquare Church

"The authors' willingness to grittily name those 'foes' of the self—arrogance, narcissism, hiding, blind spots, escapism, and others—and then accurately describe the danger these foes pose to both leaders and the led, and finally to teach the reader how to defeat each one, is what makes this book so helpful and timely."

Rick Ganz, founder and director
of the Faber Institute

"This book will be life changing for leaders of all kinds, from stay-at-home parents to megachurch pastors. The Mattsons get behind the masks to work through the core issues behind integrity gaps which will bring about healthier, higher-quality leadership at every level."

Robby Angle, president and CEO of Trueface

"Embedded within organizations and churches are leaders with unprocessed trauma and untold stories of shame. The question is not if a leader has wounds, narcissistic tendencies, or a penchant for manipulation but how committed they are to bringing those realities to light. Terra and Jeff Mattson have written a powerful work for anyone ready to face the truth of their pain before burnout or crisis strikes.

Jay Stringer, psychotherapist
and author of *Unwanted*

"Jeff and Terra have invited us to join a journey to address a gap that often exists in our personal integrity. Perhaps most of us can admit that where we are is not always consistent with what we say and how we live. As leaders we should be bold while continuing to search for God's truth regarding our own integrity journey."

Hank Danos, chairman of Danos, former
chairman of the board of supervisors at
LSU and former chairman of the Louisiana
Association of Business and Industry

"I'm excited to partner with and endorse Jeff and Terra's new book. It is ALL about leadership ... and doing it in a positive, God-fearing way that humbles the soul and gives hope to everyone who will take this journey with the Mattsons."

Neil Lomax, former NFL Arizona Cardinals
QB and 3D Coach for our future leaders

"What an insightful read that exposes the hidden pains and unique needs of being a high-capacity leader. Jeff and Terra's clinical wisdom, paired with their personal transparency, offers an empathetic but strong warning: true integrity matters."

Amy Wolff, founder of Don't Give Up Movement and co-owner of Distinction Communication Inc.

"I strongly recommend this book to leaders (influencers) of all ages because it uniquely delivers this promise: 'to discover how to mature into healthy leaders and sustain integrity over the long haul.'"

Bill Thrall, cofounder of Trueface and coauthor of *The Cure* and *The Ascent of a Leader*

"Jeff and Terra provide an in-depth framework for leaders to work through past failures, challenges, and pain, allowing them to emerge better equipped to be genuine leaders of high integrity and character. Having worked and coached in athletics for over twenty years, I have been able to observe the transformational ways great leaders can impact people. This book provides leaders with a critical foundation and skill set to model high integrity in both leadership and life."

Nick West, MS Ed., director of basketball operations for the Portland Trail Blazers

"*Shrinking the Integrity Gap* challenges readers to engage with their own personal reflections and cast a vision for who they will become. It's loaded with practical application on how to live and lead in a way that invites others to join you on mission where everyone can flourish.

Joy Roberts, cofounder of Joy of It and JOI Friendzy

"This is a powerful, practical, and spiritual roadmap and a path to integrity from two individuals who are passionate, immensely gifted, and respected in their fields."

Pete Loescher, MBA, managing director of PNC Financial Services

"Jeff and Terra have provided us with a resource grown from experience, relationships, and the honest recognition that we are all on a journey. This is not a formulaic 'how-to' book. This is an invitation to join the pilgrimage to healthy leadership and organizations for such a time as this."

Steven G. W. Moore, PhD, executive director of MJ Murdock Charitable Trust

SHRINKING

THE

INTEGRITY

GAP

JEFF & TERRA MATTSON

SHRINKING

THE

INTEGRITY

GAP

BETWEEN WHAT LEADERS PREACH & LIVE

DAVID **C** COOK

transforming lives together

SHRINKING THE INTEGRITY GAP
Published by David C Cook
4050 Lee Vance Drive
Colorado Springs, CO 80918 U.S.A.

Integrity Music Limited, a Division of David C Cook
Brighton, East Sussex BN1 2RE, England

The graphic circle C logo is a registered trademark of David C Cook.

The website addresses recommended throughout this book are offered as a
resource to you. These websites are not intended in any way to be or imply an
endorsement on the part of David C Cook, nor do we vouch for their content.

Details in some stories have been changed to protect the identities of the persons involved.

LCCN 2020937617
ISBN 978-1-4347-1261-5
eISBN 978-1-4347-1264-6

Grateful acknowledgment is made to Lynn E. Taylor and Taylor Protocols,
Inc., for permission to use content from the Core Values Index™ (CVI).

The Team: Michael Covington, Stephanie Bennett, Judy Gillispie,
Kayla Fenstermaker, James Hershberger, Susan Murdock
Cover Design: James Hershberger

Printed in the United States of America
First Edition 2020

1 2 3 4 5 6 7 8 9 10

070220

In honor of my grandfather, Dr. Gerald Bowerly,
and his sidekick, Margo, of almost seventy-three
years. He was the most important leader in my life
and finished his race well. I love you, Grandpa.

To our daughters, Adonia and Nevaeh.
More than any other, you motivate us to practice
what we preach. We are cheering you on to live
wholehearted, to run and finish your race well!

CONTENTS

FOREWORD

He has told you, O man, what is good; and what does
the LORD require of you but to do justice, and to love
kindness, and to walk humbly with your God?

Micah 6:8 (ESV)

A great deal of ink has been put to paper on the subject of leadership. We've read and taken part in many good books, articles, podcasts, and seminars, as well as many not so good. This book is different. You will not hear about vision casting, goal setting, strategic execution, delegation, reorganization, or change management—though these are worthy areas of development for leaders.

Instead, Jeff and Terra bring us face to face with the seemingly forgotten and yet essential quality for a leader to ensure a positive, abiding impact: integrity. Not just the need for it but how to begin growing and protecting our inner lives so that right living can happen and be modeled by leaders at home, at work, and in the church.

Ten years ago, as I led our church, I stopped sleeping well, couldn't shut off my mind, didn't allow myself time off, was carrying a boatload of shame, and asked myself, *How did I end up so depressed?* After counseling I realized my leadership issues were chapters 4, 5, 8, 9, 10, and 11 ... That's all!

When we read the stories of Saul and David in the Bible, we see two men who weren't terribly different from each other. They were talented young men anointed to lead, who both started well but then were tempted like everyone else. The difference was David grew as a leader by recognizing his gaps of integrity more regularly, repenting, and closing those gaps more quickly.

Shrinking the Integrity Gap is a wake-up call to leading differently, leading better, and leading in a way in which others around us are free to be their best selves because they aren't being wounded by us, their leaders.

Over the years in leadership, we have witnessed and been impacted by the train wrecks of leaders who let the gap between what they said and how they lived grow and grow. We've felt the pain and seen the injured, bleeding souls left in leaders' wakes. Regrettably, we have caused some of these ourselves.

In this book, you see the unique cumulative wisdom of Jeff and Terra come together after years of leading, counseling, and consulting business leaders. Every leader will see himself or herself exposed and inspired in these chapters. What's even better is that the Mattsons aren't just writing about integrity; they're actually committed to shrinking the gap in their own lives. As we've worked on staff in the same faith family, partnered together in various ministry opportunities, or just enjoyed each other's families and friendship, we have seen Jeff and Terra committed to walking the talk.

This is a book every young leader should commit to read over and over again with a trusted friend to examine your own health as a leader and to see whether you are shrinking the gap between what you say versus how you live. For us veterans, read this book with your team of leaders, and begin leaving legacies of abiding healthy influence.

Striving to shrink our own integrity gaps,

Bill and Kathy Towne
Pastor, Founders of Divine Threads
Rolling Hills Community Church

PREFACE

A Note about the Core Values Index

Over the years in our counseling, coaching, ministry, and organizational development work, we have utilized many clinical, relational, and business tools and assessments. We have seen the popularity of assessments come and go, depending on cultural norms and celebrity influence. Other tools are limited to specific applications. For example, some focus on individual spiritual formation and are not meant to be applied to teams or business environments. There can be a risk of harm when assessments are used for purposes outside their designed intent or without training and research. We look for the most effective tools that remain as consistent as possible over time and that use language that motivates people toward authenticity and freedom.

Although this book is not about the Core Values Index (CVI), we will unpack the wisdom of this assessment in several of the chapters. This is our tool of choice and is one way we connect antidotes in this book to the various symptoms that leaders are vulnerable to. In 2007 another mental health professional introduced us to the CVI. With a 97 percent test/retest reliability, this tool focuses on who we are and how we can live from our most authentic selves, link arms in healthy ways with people who are wired differently than us, and contribute to the greater good of our relationships at home, at work, and in the community. Over time we've seen how the CVI stands out from the rest, getting beneath personality, gender, culture, environment, age, and the highs and lows of life to our unchanging hardwired nature.

We use the CVI because it accurately identifies who people are and who they likely will be over a lifetime. The CVI helps reveal the frames in which people see the world, communicate, learn, contribute, motivate, and experience anxiety and conflict. It provides practical applications for navigating conflict between different wiring types. Because of its design—the way it quickly resonates with people and can be applied to many areas of life—the CVI is easier to integrate into and use in the daily rhythms of life. This increases the likelihood of positive transformation for leaders of all types and for their relationships with everyone in their wake.

We will refer to the CVI while unpacking some symptoms of integrity gaps, but the information provided by this assessment is supplemental. There is no pressure to do so, but if you would like to further explore the CVI for personal, mentoring, or professional purposes, join us at www.livingwholehearted.com to take the CVI or connect with our team.

INTRODUCTION

A leader is a person who must take special responsibility for what's
going on inside him- or herself, inside his or her consciousness,
lest the act of leadership create more harm than good.
—Parker Palmer, *Leading from Within*

(Terra) I picked up the phone and could sense the despondency
of the caller. At twenty-one years old, I was interning at the counseling center of a prominent Christian ministry by taking free
counseling calls from around the nation. The pastor on the line
begged to remain anonymous and said he had nowhere else to turn.
In utter despair, he confessed that he was having an affair and was
ready to end his life. He felt trapped and uncertain about how he
had landed in his tangled mess. When I started my internship, I
held the false ideal that leaders, especially those who loved Jesus,
did not struggle like others. The saddest part was that his call was
one of many similar ones I would take over those months. What I
unpacked that day with this pastor was the beginning of a lifetime
of work with Jeff to help leaders bring integrity to the most hidden
parts of their stories.

Recent years have seen more examples of the fallout from individuals failing to live and lead with integrity. Is integrity real? Is it
important? Integrity is highly valued but rarely lived out. Can it even
be achieved? If so, is there anyone actually living and leading with

integrity who can model the way? Unfortunately, the answers to these questions today might be different than we think.

In fact, integrity is not about managing all the hats you wear, mastering a set of tools, or somehow achieving enlightened perfection. Integrity is a commitment to shrinking the gap between the values you preach and live. For leaders, integrity is a process of allowing ourselves and others to be human. Rather than hiding behind the masks of achievement, influence, and status, we engage in the process of learning to live and lead with greater congruence and grace.

A leader is anyone who has a following, and how you lead matters. If you have children, you are a leader. If you run a *Fortune* 500 company, you are a leader. Leaders come in all shapes and sizes, but they have some commonalities that are rarely discussed among leaders at the top of organizations. This book is for high-capacity leaders as well as those healing from leaders who lacked integrity, those working with leaders (coaches and counselors), and, of course, emerging leaders.

Sometimes a leader is the charismatic, type-A, driven, goal-oriented achiever who commits years to building things and making things happen. These leaders are the movers, the shakers, and often the ones others in the room look to. These are pioneer types who find themselves further up the ladder every time they turn around. Other leaders may have never wanted leadership but find themselves being handed responsibility they didn't bargain for and fumbling to steward their influence. They may be quiet and reserved leaders who provide clear structure and protocols but lack warmth. Sometimes leaders are selected simply because of their skills, education, or flash and are placed on a pedestal of leadership without actually being ready for the role. For example, Saul of the Old Testament was chosen to be Israel's first king based primarily on his looks and stature. His selfish ambitions and jealousy eventually overtook his leadership, creating a ripple effect of consequences (see 1 Sam. 9–10). Though leadership roles are filled with a variety of personalities, the focus of this book is not how to be a leader but rather what we do with the influence we are given and how to become leaders of integrity along the way.

Imagine leadership in our lives taking on a new definition as we lead from who we are rather than from our agendas, accomplishments, or the image we work to preserve. **Imagine leadership where we allow ourselves to be seen, known, and even loved. Then imagine offering the same authentic experience to those we directly influence in our homes, our organizations, and our communities. Wholehearted Leaders bring all of who they are—mind, body, soul, and relationships—before God and others to live free from hiding and mature in humility and honesty.**

This is a different kind of leadership book. Not one with easy five-step plans, magic, or fluff. Instead, this book calls us into the deep end of the pool to discover how to mature into healthy leaders and sustain integrity over the long haul. We will unpack integrity. What does it mean, how is it obtained, and how is it lived out in practical ways so we can all experience more leaders who finish their race well? A leader with integrity is not perfect by any means. Rather, leaders with integrity know who they are and understand their own stories, wiring, and limitations. These leaders can receive feedback, see themselves as part of the greater work of their teams, and remain grounded in grace-filled relationships with those outside the groups they lead. **This leader understands that integrity is not just a word but a way of being.**

God had both of us noticing leaders from an early age—in our family systems, in our schools, then in our churches during our elementary years, until He eventually put us in leadership positions. Today we run a counseling practice and organizational development firm serving leaders, their families, and the businesses and ministries they run throughout the Pacific Northwest and beyond. On the counseling side, Terra leads a team of mental health professionals who provide quality counseling for couples, individuals, teens, and children, integrating the latest in trauma, neurobiology, spiritual formation, and family systems from a biblical worldview. On the organizational development side, Jeff and his team are invited to work with leaders and their teams to help them thrive and solve the people issues that keep them up at night. Together, striving to *help leaders live with integrity*, we are known as Living Wholehearted.

Though our expertise comes from our research and professional years in the trenches with high-achieving leaders, their families, and their organizations, we are leaders ourselves. Many have shaped our thinking and the way we try (as our friends at Trueface like to say) to let our theology influence our reality. C. S. Lewis may have said it best: "I believe in Christianity as I believe that the Sun has risen, not only because I see it, but because by it I see everything else."[1] The work we do as husband and wife is not just a job for us; it's a passion and a deep call that is infused into every area of our lives. It is essential for us to live what we teach. That's hard, and we don't do it perfectly, but even if no one is watching, our marriage and parenting are better for it. Our leadership roles cross many spheres:

raising our two daughters, running a counseling and consulting business, writing, and speaking. We influence—and are influenced by—a community of friends, our extended family, our church, and our local community, including our kids' volleyball, basketball, and soccer teams. Like you, we've got skin in the game, and the journey is critically important.

After twenty years of helping leaders inside churches, parachurch ministries, businesses, and other organizations, we see a clear and unfortunate trend. Each generation of leaders inherits the toxic baggage of previous generations and then passes on that baggage if it goes unaddressed. This includes burnout, hiding, wearing masks, creating unsafe systems, and perpetuating abuse. Emerging research supports that high achievers are often compartmentalized and emotionally detached survivors of abuse. We are in the midst of a crisis.

However, there is hope. Not all leaders with trauma compartmentalize. Consider Joseph of the Bible. Joseph's leadership journey became rooted in trauma when his brothers dumped him into a pit and sold him into slavery. After years of suffering, Joseph accelerated into leadership because of his gifts and eventually was promoted to a position of great power. Through God, he faced the wounds from his childhood and refined his leadership. In an unusual set of circumstances, God brought Joseph's abusers (his brothers) back into his life. Only this time Joseph was in a position to use his power to bring help or harm to them; he chose to help (see Gen. 37–47). This begs the question, How does a leader finish well regardless of how his or her story began?

Dr. J. Robert Clinton, a seasoned professor of leadership at Fuller Seminary, "believes that more than 70 percent of leaders do not finish well." He bases this statistic on six criteria of leaders who do not finish well:

1. They lose their learning posture—no longer listening and growing.
2. The attractiveness of their character wanes.
3. They stop living by their convictions.
4. They fail to leave behind ultimate contributions.
5. They stop walking in awareness of their influence and destiny.
6. They lose their once-vibrant relationship with God.[2]

We think one of the major revelations from Dr. Clinton's work is that high-functioning leaders—at the top of many org charts—often suffer from unresolved trauma and tragic childhoods. In fact, to survive abuse, a person must have a high tolerance for intensity and a low awareness of boundaries, resulting in higher thresholds for stress. Using maladaptive coping strategies rooted in early trauma, many leaders compartmentalize their own vulnerable needs (and the needs of those they care about) and carry heavier loads than most. Most trauma survivors take one of two roads: the performer or the victim. Sometimes leaders can be the performer at work and the victim at home. Or maybe they refuse to ever be the victim again, so performer is the only real option. Sadly, many leaders develop a pattern of numbing out with more socially acceptable vices like workaholism, performance-based achievements, and the never-ending drive to innovate. This cycle must stop because the wreckage from shattered trust is far too great!

Is there a better coping strategy than achievement and success? For many, performance and achievement have resulted in rewards and attention—an overcomer's success story. This may be entirely healthy and a positive outcome. But achievement and success have allowed others to hide, avoid pain, or keep from looking back for fear of shame, uncontrollable emotions, or paralysis. We have found ourselves in the same tempting trap of achievement and success and know the subtleness of its hooks.

Leadership itself can create a unique form of trauma most don't recognize until it's too late. **Leaders are usually unaware of how their desire to compartmentalize pain and earlier trauma drives their need to perform.** The wearying burdens of long hours, decision-making, critical feedback, and increasing responsibility negatively impact their lives and the lives of those they influence by wearing on family relationships, affecting health, and creating severe loneliness.

We want to make a dent in the wake of systemic abuse by *shrinking the integrity gap*. *Abuse* seems like such a heavy word choice here, and you might stop and wonder whether this book is for you. Please know that many of us are unaware of the abuse in our lives or the tendencies we have in our own relationships. Abusive behaviors can be the result of our wider gaps without us ever being abusers. We will unpack this idea in certain chapters, but for many, this word choice resonates far too deeply. Please continue with us, as we have much to share that will help you be the leader you want to be. The cycle can be stopped by leaders who are ready to live and lead in a different direction: shrinking their integrity gaps and stewarding their influence for the sake of others. We seek to not only identify the problem of failed leadership, its root-level causes, and its destructive effects; we also provide a framework for young emerging leaders to engage in the necessary work of shrinking their personal integrity gaps. Living and leading with integrity is attainable and benefits every aspect of life—from personal to professional.

By taking the inward journey of considering several key factors—such as family of origin, faith/worldview development, traumatic events, hardwired nature, and character development—leaders can understand what is impacting their integrity. **Emerging leaders can get their baggage down to carry-on size** before landing the dream job with money, title, and power that might falsely guarantee satisfaction.

Our goal is to see more healthy and integrated leaders emerge into and influence the work world and the sacred institutions that need them most. These are what we call Wholehearted Leaders: those who lead without using people in order to get their own unresolved needs met. These leaders, the real deal, are leading from a place of authentic personhood to help meet the needs of those they serve.

We are going to unpack the common factors that prevent wholehearted leadership: burnout, poor listening, arrogance, isolation, ignoring one's own needs, ignoring family needs, dismissing the value of others' contributions, narcissism, moral failures, and more. The seasoned leader who resonates with any of these symptoms of an integrity gap will find practical next steps and hope in targeted antidotes for each symptom, along with tools for walking with those they mentor. When applied with consistency over time, these antidotes can help you stay on track—or get back on track if you've slightly veered or faced a full-on derailment!

We personally invite you to join our movement. At the end of chapters 3–12, we provide key markers. As you read these key markers, note that they may relate to you or a leader in your life. Our use of the word *you* could stand for *he* or *she*. These lists are not exhaustive nor meant to be used to shame or diagnose. We simply want to show some identifiable markers to help us all look at our own integrity gaps along the way. We also provide antidotes—next steps to consider—as you engage your own integrity gap.

Consider using this book with your teams or in safe mentoring relationships. The book itself is a guide to deeper relationship with God, yourself, and a trusted few so you have an environment to process your experiences well. As we later address, one of the best things to do if you are struggling and feel unsure how to get help is to begin processing with a competent Christian counselor. We have plenty of stories to tell from our own lives. We have our own gaps, have been hurt by leaders without integrity, and have walked with leaders who led and finished their races well. We want to help you integrate the reality of this message into every part of who you are. We know what it's like to slip off the road of integrity, to be helped up, and then to step back onto the narrow path of shrinking the integrity gap. We are looking ahead for our own daughters and the generations to come.

Let's live and lead from integrity. Healthy relationships and character do matter. Let's change the course of leadership so that more leaders are who they say they are, resulting in more healthy relationships everywhere.

Helping leaders live with integrity,
Jeff & Terra

Part I

UNDERSTANDING LEADERSHIP
AND INTEGRITY GAPS

Chapter 1

FOUNDATIONS OF LEADING

All a person's ways seem pure to them, but
motives are weighed by the LORD.

—Proverbs 16:2

In our offices as counselors and executive coaches, we encounter the leaders behind the masks. Stories that would shock most no longer faze us, as we have become accustomed to the human impulse to live a divided life. Sadly, addiction and betrayal are more normal than not among high-level leaders both inside and outside the church. Years ago, a successful Christian businessman landed himself in jail one night after he was caught in a police sting of men soliciting prostitutes. The next morning, people woke to the news that the beloved husband, father, grandfather, boss, Christian leader, and generous philanthropist wasn't who they had known him to be. He was living a divided life. The fallout was massive and affected hundreds of lives directly and indirectly. It took years before people would begin to trust him again, as he worked to shrink his integrity gap through repentance, professional help, and letting others walk with him along the road of healing. He had to face the reality of the pit he had dug and fallen into, taking those he loved with him. With God's help and by His grace, he eventually began to climb out.

31

This story and similar ones belong to hundreds of our clients. A well-known lawyer and Christian leader is accused in a serial sex-abuse case within his church community. In denial and leveraging a carefully cultivated reputation, this sex offender is left to lead in the church while the survivors are not believed and are accused of mental illness, bitterness, and a lack of forgiveness. A wife shares how lonely and belittled she feels by her well-loved and adored husband, who leads many in the church they founded as young believers. The community sees him as a pillar of wisdom, and she wonders who will believe her when she can no longer watch him neglect their marriage for the sake of the greater good—a family sacrificed on the altar of ministry. A nonprofit leader finds herself burning the candle at both ends and abusing prescription drugs to get through her days. Substance abuse was never on her list of vices as she was growing up in youth group, but she cannot seem to shake the need for the pills in order to get through her days with all the demands of her to-do list.

These stories are unfortunately more common than many realize. When individuals are exposed, people often say things such as "How can this be? He was so nice!" "She was a Sunday school teacher for twenty years!" "He has such a great family!" "We all loved her." We are tired of seeing people shrug their shoulders with incredulous indifference. It is time for change. No one gets to these significant moments overnight. Instead, the constant drip of a leaking faucet is ignored until the whole house is flooded. We see early warning signs, but we have become accustomed to ignoring them until there's a full-blown disaster.

DEFINING INTEGRITY

Living a life of integrity begins with valuing character over riches and power, recognizing that as God's creation all people are on a level playing field, and foreseeing danger with humility and a healthy fear of the Lord. When we know who we are and to whom we belong (God), then we pay better attention to the leaking faucets. Proverbs provides wisdom for those of us who want to grow in awareness:

> Choose a good reputation over great riches;
> > being held in high esteem is better than silver
> > or gold.
> The rich and poor have this in common:
> > The LORD made them both.
> A prudent person foresees danger and takes
> > precautions.
> The simpleton goes blindly on and suffers the
> > consequences.
> True humility and fear of the LORD
> > lead to riches, honor, and long life.
> Corrupt people walk a thorny, treacherous road;
> > whoever values life will avoid it. (22:1–5 NLT)

Let's consider some key questions. Why would people live hidden lives that are completely at odds with who others think they are? Why would they desperately try to get away with it? Why is it that so many leaders in every sphere (education, business, government, the church,

medicine, sports and entertainment, etc.) fall into the pattern of success
followed by moral failure and catastrophic fallout, followed by years of
denial, blame, and little repair? Why would young men and women
want to be people of influence when the news cycle every day features
leaders getting caught cheating, lying, stealing, preying on vulnerable
populations, covering their tracks, hoarding wealth, and bragging about
it? Can we choose integrity? Is it possible to attain, let alone preserve?

So many of these leaders causing wounds and pain are professed
followers of Jesus and sit in positions of authority as lead pastors,
elders, and C-suite executives. They are likely respected and unaware
of how they are affecting others. In Matthew 12:25 Jesus "knew their
thoughts and said to them, 'Every kingdom divided against itself
will be ruined, and every city or household divided against itself will
not stand.'" A leader divided cannot stand, and we have continually found those words to be true. The wounds and pain can come
quickly, but the healing does not.

A way to look at integrity is as every part of your life—mind,
heart, soul, actions, and relationships—moving in the same direction
(hopefully a God-designed direction). Parker Palmer said integrity is
"much more than adherence to a moral code." It means "'the state
or quality of being entire, complete, and unbroken,' as in *integer* or
integral. Deeper still, integrity refers to something … in its 'unim-
paired, unadulterated, or genuine state, corresponding to its original
condition.' When we understand integrity for what it is, we stop
obsessing over codes of conduct and embark on the more demanding
journey toward being whole."[1]

Who is a leader? To boil it down, a leader is anyone with a
following. **Leadership is a relationship word.** *Merriam-Webster*

says the word *lead* means "to guide on a way especially by going in advance."[2] Of course, if you are leading a corporation, you have hundreds (maybe thousands) of people following you. But what if you are a single parent with two kids in diapers? We would argue that you are leading one of the most important organizations on the planet … the family unit.

UNCOVERING THE INTEGRITY GAP

How you live and lead matters, whether you're the CEO of a *Fortune* 500 company, a manager at Trader Joe's, the youth pastor at a local church, or the pope himself! An integrity gap is the distance between the values we preach (what we say about ourselves and want others to believe about us) and the values we actually live out (in front of people or when no one sees). When leaders of all types *live* and *lead* with integrity, everyone in their wake benefits; when an integrity gap exists, everyone in their wake pays … it's just a matter of time. Living as Wholehearted Leaders—whose character and inner life match external life—directly benefits everyone.

Whose leadership wake have you been in, and how did this person's leadership and integrity (or lack thereof) impact you? For some, a name and face immediately came into focus. Perhaps this leader influenced you in numerous positive ways, inspiring you to grow to your potential. But perhaps you survived abuse from this person (a family member or a previously trusted pastor, coach, or teacher). Perhaps you thought everything was pretty great in your life until you got news from your parents that you would soon be a divorce statistic. Perhaps you had a boss who always got his or her way, belittled you in front of your colleagues, or told you to compromise your standards or else. Maybe it's the pastor you serve alongside who talks poorly of others but then does an about-face when in public.

> There are no shortcuts to developing character and integrity—a wholehearted life.

It may take time to identify the leaders in your life who really affected you and may still be affecting you. If you've spent years (even decades) trying to block out the past, chances are you may have forgotten a few details and will need more than a few days to recall them. If you feel the question is not worth evaluating because the main issue is not really about how anyone has affected you (as if someone could) but about how you're affecting others, then this book is for you too.

There are no shortcuts to developing character and integrity—a wholehearted life. It takes real guts and grit to jump into the deep end and stay there to uncover where our pain, fears, false beliefs, and unhealthy coping strategies were birthed. But the deep end is also where healing, integrity, character, and healthy leadership emerge. In *The Road to Character*, David Brooks included this passage from an email he received: "The heart cannot be taught in a classroom intellectually, to students mechanically taking notes.... Good, wise hearts are obtained through lifetimes of diligent effort to dig deeply within and heal lifetimes of scars.... You can't teach it or email it or tweet it. It has to be discovered within the depths of one's own heart when a person is finally ready to go looking for it, and not before."[3]

EMERGING LEADERS

We recognize that many reading this book are young and emerging leaders. You have not yet reached your greatest level of influence in terms of status, money, and power because of your stage of life. Nothing would give us greater joy than for high school and under-graduate students to read this clinical, biblical, and relational wisdom and apply it to their lives right now! We are rooting for you. *You can have a greater impact on your life and career (from a time and resource standpoint) if you work now to get your baggage down to carry-on size. You will lead from a more authentic place, knowing that the road ahead is not easy nor pain-proof.* Time is on your side when you put away money early and let it grow. Similar to the power of compound inter-est, the more you invest now in being a Wholehearted Leader, the less catching up and correcting you'll have to do later. "The advantages are even greater for someone making regular contributions to the investment."[4] Integrating this wisdom into your young life is worth your investment now.

In 1 Timothy 4:12, the apostle Paul told a younger pastor he was mentoring, "Don't let anyone look down on you because you are young, but set an example for the believers in speech, in conduct, in love, in faith and in purity." Paul was edifying this younger man, whom many say may have been in his early thirties, to teach and serve through modeling integrity. Age did not matter. Paul encour-aged him to lead by example with his words, actions, love, faith, and purity. We are saying to you, emerging leaders, it is possible to learn from those who have gone before us. Slow down and examine your "why" and your "ways" in order to set a trajectory that will take you to the finish line.

(Jeff) When we were newly married and in our early twenties, Terra had a personal goal to run a marathon. Me—not so much. As a track runner in my early years, I had been there and done that. But I was committed to helping her finish the race well.

One of the lessons Terra learned was that her training made all the difference in how she ran her race and how she felt days later. She was committed to doing the hard work a whole year in advance. By the time she ran her first (and only) marathon, she enjoyed the entire race and did not have the same fatigue other runners experienced. Her commitment to working hard on the front end paid dividends on the back end. Similar to Terra, emerging leaders who want to lead well will follow a training regimen in order to run the race well.

You may have a passion to change from the way things were done in your family, to create a different kind of legacy. You may have survived a journey made difficult by a leader or leaders with large integrity gaps. You've been waiting for someone who loves Jesus and the church to say that something is wrong ... that there's a systemic problem with way too many leaders in ministry and with leaders in general. We hope this book will be like a breath of fresh air.

You may have vast wealth, influence, and power. Some of you (not all) in this category may be feeling uncomfortable with what you have read so far because you know you have a wider integrity gap than most know. You might struggle with ambivalence because you like things about your gap and at the same time you don't like it. This is a common place to be as a leader.

Maybe you're a high-profile pastor of a megachurch or a Christian entertainer who's successfully grown a following from the tens to the tens of thousands. You've got all the pressure of the CEO of a publicly traded *Fortune* 500 company. You're also a publicly known Christian and may feel the weight of maintaining the reputation of God, which is only His to uphold. That is an enormous amount of pressure that no one talks about until after the fall.

Some of you are still enjoying the climb up the ladder, while others have become depressed, disillusioned, and weary of being lonely at the top—even with King Solomon–like wealth, influence, and power. We're glad you have felt some dissonance inside as you've read to this point. The good news is that you can still do something about the gap that feels so wide right now.

> Shame is a powerful tool of the Enemy to keep us hiding, clawing, and drowning in our own narratives.

The longer you put off change, the more people in your wake are being negatively affected whether you see it or not. Shame is a powerful tool of the Enemy to keep us hiding, clawing, and drowning in our own narratives. Jesus said the truth will set us free (see John 8:32). Facing the truth of who we are, what we have done, and how we impact others is hard work, but you and those you lead are worth it! To the Christian pastor, elder, artist, or CEO, the good news remains that only Jesus saves, and His reputation remains in His hands, not in yours or mine.

SEASONED LEADERS

Finally, some of you reading this book are seasoned leaders who are thriving and are already working on closing your gaps. We hope you will utilize this text in your mentoring relationships. We also want to acknowledge those of you who had status, power, wealth, and more and lost it all, whether through moral failure or burnout. You somehow survived but barely. We feel for you too. You may have tremendous remorse for the choices you made and the consequences you put others through. You've come to the place (or are close to it) where you have owned what was yours to own. You are letting God handle the matter with perfect justice in His timing, not yours. If you have dedicated the balance of your life to helping others not make the same mistakes, to helping them experience the grace and forgiveness they desperately need, we invite you to use this book to inspire and encourage the next generation of leaders and influencers within your sphere.

Thank you for having the courage to face your own story, recognizing that there is a difference between using power appropriately and inappropriately and that abuse (whether verbal, physical, sexual, spiritual, or through neglect) has no place in God's house or any house. We celebrate your pursuit of living more integrated and becoming the kind of leader you would follow—getting the help you need, staying in hope, and changing the system you are in or came from so others can do more than just survive.

Although God doesn't wish for any leader to fall into sin and despair (see John 10:10), your story can have a powerful and redemptive side. Those who go through the long and difficult journey of healing can have a larger impact post-failure than they ever imagined. Your story can give you credibility in the eyes of those who need your example. That is grace! Doing the hard work of repair can lead to redemption on so many levels because most people won't give you access to their lives unless you prove your reliability. When you can be honest about your whole journey, it provides a beautiful road map for others. Kouzes and Posner said credibility is "what people demand of their leaders as a prerequisite to willingly contributing their hearts and minds to a common cause."[5] Bringing your whole story to the table builds trustworthiness and can be a game changer for other leaders.

It's never too late to shrink our integrity gaps. One leader with global impact for good, after an initially negative impact, was Charles Colson. He is remembered for helping Nixon with Watergate. Colson spent seven months in prison, but in the following decades, he founded and led a ministry called Prison Fellowship. Furthermore, he went on to author thirty books and produce a radio broadcast called *BreakPoint* with more than 1,400 outlets. Yes, Watergate is a part of Colson's legacy, but even so, the consistent, positive, and powerful influence of his life post-Watergate is indisputable.

Consider whom you might invite into your own journey. Do not stop here. We are just getting started, and we believe this might be a turning point in your story if you are willing and ready for the ride.

Antidotes

1. Consider reading this book with one or two other people, and allow yourself to be truly honest. You may want to read this book with your leadership team as well to help shape the health of your team.

2. Make a list of characteristics you see in great leaders. Why do you believe these qualities to be what defines a great leader? Who has had the biggest role in getting you to the place of influence you are in or are heading toward?

3. Consider why you would want to shrink your integrity gap. Why would you invest time and energy in this part of your leadership? Write a short statement and put it somewhere you can reference so you do not forget along the way. *The people I serve deserve integrity / My kids*

4. Why do you think God has given you leadership qualities? Reflect and journal about His purpose for influence.

integrity
responsible
pro-active
empathetic
authentic
humble
wise - or wisdom seeking

Chapter 2

STORIES OF LEADING

Experience is a brutal teacher.
But you learn—my God, do you learn.
—C. S. Lewis, *Shadowlands*

Before we go any further, we want to share some of our own stories and the integrity gaps we are trying to shrink through honesty, dependence on grace, mentorship, and love for one another and our kids (just to mention a few characteristics).

(Jeff) In my youth I was caught up in the tsunamis of multiple leaders in my life who did not live with integrity. As a young adult I was largely unaware that I was living with the consequences of others' integrity gaps and sin. I'll get to my family of origin later, but during my four years of high school, I had four different youth pastors at my home church, a mainline evangelical church in a booming suburb of Portland, Oregon. Although we were never told the details of why Pastor A was "transitioning out," it never sat well with me or many of my peers. The sniffer was out and something stank. I'd later learn that in several instances my sniffer was unfortunately right. For example, one youth pastor of a crosstown church I used to visit with friends went to prison after he was found guilty of molesting a girl in his youth group. If something stinks, there's a good chance you're smelling something rotten.

Unfortunately, way too many leaders in the church and in parachurch ministries are moved around and don't get the help they need, leaving victims unprotected. Has this happened so much that we've become numb to it?

Friends of ours, Steve and Celestia Tracy, founded Mending the Soul, a ministry that helps churches understand the frequency of abuse: the Scriptures speak of it because it's possible for any of us to be abused or an abuser, particularly those given power. Steve has said, "Few Christians, even Christian leaders, truly believe abuse is rampant through all segments of society and is even committed by Christian leaders. Over and over, parents, congregations, and religious leaders deny abuse reports, regardless of the weight of the evidence."[1]

JEFF'S MINISTRY STORY

Twenty years ago I was a fresh college grad with my educational ministry degree and youth ministry minor from a well-respected Christian liberal arts university. I was about to start my first week in full-time ministry at a church in downtown Seattle. I was so excited to do great things for God (ah, the humility) and for so many underprivileged men, women, and children in the city. We bussed in kids every Sunday for kids' church because mom, dad, or grandma didn't have a car; we ran a homeless shelter and clothing closet to meet basic needs; we hosted a traveling trailer and ministry team to share the gospel in parks. People were getting saved everywhere … *Bam!* We had it all except money and extra hours in the day! There I was, a white suburban kid ready to serve in a teen center in the heart of the urban community. Our pastor, John, and his wife were third-generation missionaries from Indonesia who had seen real persecution for being Christian. They were tested, tried, and true, but I was not.

I drew on my own experience in church youth culture, which was fun, exciting, inviting, and affluent. I grew up in a middle- to upper-middle-class family where both my parents worked, my siblings and I never wanted for much (food, shelter, clothing), and we took vacations. My parents dropped hundreds of dollars for me to attend church camp every year (in addition to sports camps). When it came time to recruit kids to our summer church camp, it was a hard sell to get fourteen kids—twelve of whom spoke English as their second language—motivated about the idea of going into the woods for a week with strangers.

Once most of the kids were on board, it was time to start raising money to make ends meet. I had participated in a ton of camp fund-raisers in my day, and at the top of my list was the standard car wash! I worked with the owner of a local gas station and secured the chance to promote and run a car wash on an early-summer day. We had buckets, soap, hoses, and signs to pull this puppy off and raise a bunch of money to get to camp. The kids put in some serious sweat equity! Car after car pulled into the lot as we rotated who was on the corner holding signs and who was washing cars. After hours of action in the heat, the sun was beginning to go down and the kids were beat. I remember yelling, "One more car, you guys. Then we're done!" Within a minute or so, that final car came and we all worked together to finish it.

Less than thirty seconds after I uttered "One more car, you guys …" *Pop! Pop! Pop! … Pop! Pop! Pop! Pop!* The shots were deafening. The kids started screaming, and some dropped to the ground at the familiar sounds. A car had pulled up at the intersection we were working, and the driver got out and began shooting at the car in front of him. The driver of the front car was shot and died before our eyes with his body hanging halfway out of the car onto the pavement. I realized that if the kids had not moved seconds earlier, they would have been hit by a car or bullets. Like standing waist deep in the ocean, **I felt as if my feet were getting yanked out from beneath me. The undertow grabbed me, and a voice in my head whispered, "Welcome to ministry."**

I tell this story to make the point that although I still believe God called me to that position, I was so naive, unaware, and unprepared. No ministry classes could have prepared me for the road that lay ahead. What I'm going to tell you next is equally shocking and painful.

MINISTRY WITH RICH

The church where I began my long-awaited first vocational ministry position had been at that Seattle location since the early 1940s. Even with a history dating back to 1917, it no longer exists. The primary reason the church closed its doors is rooted in the story of Rich and his integrity gap.

Rich was my first ministry boss and was a gregarious kind of guy. He had moved from California and arrived on the scene five years before me. He liked the city, apparently had gifts in business administration, and ultimately convinced our pastor, John, and his wife that he could help them with the kingdom work they were endeavoring to do. When I was hired, only a few families and individuals were regularly tithing. Money was not the focus of the church, and if we needed to do something for hurting people, we knew God would provide in some amazing way. To make a greater impact on our city and on the lives of those we served in our community, we needed a savvy businessperson to help steward and develop the limited resources God entrusted to us. A full-time position was eventually created for Rich, and he became the church administrator.

About a year into my role as youth pastor, I got to work one day, and everyone on our small staff was wondering where Rich was, as no one had heard from him. It was really unusual not to see him there first thing in the morning. After we were unable to contact his wife, Nelly, we began to get concerned that something had happened to him on his commute. A team drove to Rich and Nelly's home. The rest of us began to work and waited hopefully for an update that all was well.

What I soon found out made my stomach drop. I can feel it even as I write today. The search team reached Nelly, and she gave my colleagues access to a hidden key to their house. They found it empty, and Rich's wedding ring was on the master-bedroom dresser. It didn't make any sense.

Hours went by with no word from Rich, and then Pastor John called a meeting. As I read his body language and noticed the dread in his eyes, I tried to prepare myself for the worst. "We don't know where Rich is, but we know that my signature was forged and our bank accounts have been emptied." The confusion was palpable. I asked, "Did Rich steal from us and abandon his wife and all of us?" He answered with clarity: "Yes, it appears that is what has happened." Once more I felt the undertow and heard, **"Welcome to ministry."**

Processing this in later years, I learned more about what seminary professor and abuse expert Steve Tracy said in his book *Mending the Soul*: "Abusers are often very cunning, and they deceitfully prey on the very virtues of those they abuse, counting on the fact that their victims will not act treacherously, as they do."[2] I have not forgotten those profound moments and the lessons they have taught me.

All of us wondered, *What do we do now?* Pastor John and his wife shared, with great love for their staff, that while this investigation was in process, there would be no funds to pay salaries. They suggested we all get second jobs in order to keep the church doors open for the disadvantaged we served. The responses in the room ranged from shock, disgust, hurt, and anger to many, many tears. What happened next was a leadership moment I won't forget. John ended the meeting by simply and honestly asking God to help us (and particularly Nelly) through this. He prayed for Rich to confess, repent, and find healing for whatever he was battling that had led him to do something like this.

John didn't have to include Rich in his simple prayer. But this man had seen the presence of evil in the persecution of Christian men, women, and children in Sumatra, Indonesia—the belly of radical Islamic terrorism. Because his family had lived through this evil, he knew when Satan was at work. He also knew who terrified Satan—the Lord Jesus Christ!

In a matter of days, the police followed the money and found Rich in Las Vegas spending everything he had stolen. The police required an audit in order to formally pursue and prosecute Rich. As the church had literally no money left in the bank accounts, Pastor John focused on how to pay the utilities at the end of that month. Ultimately, he and his wife decided to release Rich to the One who would judge him perfectly and whom Rich could not run from. Their gesture reminded me of what Desmond Tutu once said: "To forgive is not just to be altruistic. It is the best form of self-interest. What dehumanizes you inexorably dehumanizes me. It gives people resilience, enabling them to survive and emerge still human despite all efforts to dehumanize them."[3]

I had a clear call to this faith community, and I believed in our work. I truly wanted to help during this crisis, so I remained in ministry while adding a side job in order to pay the bills. Not all the other staff members felt the same, and I do not blame them. In fact, the day Pastor John first shared the news was the same day several of our small staff of eleven packed up their belongings and left without saying good-bye. I resonated with their feelings and decision to get out, but I didn't understand at the time why they didn't say good-bye after hundreds of hours "all in" together and after witnessing what many of us truly believed to be miracles (like our protection at the car wash!). Looking back, I see that this ordeal caused a level of trauma bonding, like the bonding that soldiers experience during war, as we ventured into the wake of Rich's betrayal.

As if that wasn't traumatic enough, we later found out the same man who had taught workshops on integrity and preached the gospel from the pulpit was a master manipulator who preyed on naivete. He was in fact a professional embezzler who had defrauded another church in California years before he landed in Seattle and probably had an extensive history of manipulation, sex addiction, and criminal behavior. This is a key vulnerability for churches who "forgive and forget" because of Christ's grace: not thoroughly looking into a person's background and believing what the person says when no track record or community can confirm his or her character. I won't forget the pain on Nelly's face as she sobbed at Rich's desk after porn was discovered on his church computer—right next to a picture of them as a couple. Rich was gone. Friends and colleagues were gone. Everyone around me was hurting. **Welcome to ministry.**

This was a new level of pain for me. Although something felt oddly familiar, I wouldn't put my finger on it for years. There I was in my early twenties, seeking to "do the Lord's work" by loving fourteen kids and attempting to understand what had happened while trying not to lose hope. It was a struggle! To be honest, I was losing faith, hope, and love. Terra, who was a student at the university I had just graduated from, was interning for me. We both had a passion for youth ministry and had been dating for a while. Between the two of us, we were actually loving these kids well, seeing them grow and lean into their own relationships with God. I thought if Terra and I could make it through that car wash, then we could make it through anything. However, the ambivalence, the pain, and the struggle to get past Rich's betrayal became too big for me. I began to drown, and I felt like I wasn't going to make it.

TRAUMA AND PTSD

(Terra) Our staff had experienced a traumatic event. We often think of trauma as something like a school shooting or a parent leaving. Many define it more narrowly, such as getting hit as a child or suffering sexual abuse. However, the definition of *trauma* is broader than we think, and trauma affects more of us than we imagine. Neuroscience and the newer research around the impact of the digital age have created a broader definition of *trauma* as "anything less than nurturing." **Trauma is anything out of the ordinary that leaves us feeling helpless and powerless.** A sense of powerlessness can descend after someone survives an experience such as an earthquake, a violent conflict between his or her parents, being humiliated in front of others, or being uprooted from a familiar home. These types of experiences leave a person, especially one in an inferior position of power, feeling out of control. To survive, the person develops maladaptive or dysfunctional coping strategies that offer much-needed feelings of safety and security and create a false way to meet God-given needs. Many individuals have experienced compounded trauma, where experiences from various parts of their journey created a larger impact over time.

To be clear, not all traumas create posttraumatic stress disorder. According to the *Diagnostic and Statistical Manual of Mental Disorders* (DSM-5), PTSD results from "exposure to actual or threatened death, serious injury, or sexual violence."[4] The definition of *threatened death or serious injury* varies based on the perspective of the survivor's age and power position. Size, gender, position, and cultural norms also influence what is filed in the brain as potential danger. In fact, in the digital age of violent video games, pornography, cyberbullying, suicide, and live feeds of violence, the average person's experience of perceived harm has increased. To allow our stories to be heard and processed, our definition of *trauma* must expand.

God created our brains in a way that helps us prepare for and react to danger. Preventing PTSD is most contingent on what happens after traumatic events and whether people find comfort and care as they process their narratives of the events. In his book *The Body Keeps the Score: Brain, Mind, and Body in the Healing of Trauma*, clinician and trauma researcher Bessel van der Kolk explained that when the mind and the body become overwhelmed, a person develops patterns and strategies to help him or her perceive danger and increase the likelihood of survival. When a person is unable to talk about the realities of his or her experience, emotions, and perceptions with a safe and trusted other, the brain files the traumatic event under the subtitle "Never Let This Happen Again!" This automatic fight, flight, or freeze system serves us well when we are in emergency situations. However, similar to a car in park with the engine on and the gas pedal pressed to the floor, someone who has not processed his or her traumatic stories begins to store energy in his or her body with no outlet. The body remembers even if we cognitively forget.[5]

THE FALLOUT

(Jeff) As the shock of Rich's actions began to wear off, reality set in. Rich's abandonment hit deep for all of us, but it really cut the fourteen kids in our youth group. Growing up in an impoverished part of Seattle, they had been taught many more hard life lessons than I had been exposed to at twice their age! The harshness of their lives might not have been obvious in the hallways of their public schools, but they were often silenced, hungry, and forced to take on the roles and responsibilities of adults. To see them in their homes, it was as if a switch were flipped as their guard went up and they coped. I had wanted to create safe and fun environments where they could laugh, cry, question, learn, and use their voices. I longed for them to see and experience Jesus' love, care, and practical provision for them, to know that with Him, all things were possible for them.

> We may have to live with the consequences of someone else's sin even if we did not commit the sin ourselves.

The moment I shared the news with the youth, their faces fell and they wouldn't look me in the eye. It was as if they had expected a letdown to come from me at some point. I cannot put words to the hurt I felt as I delivered that news, and even worse was seeing the kids withdraw their trust from me, even though I was not the perpetrator. I would pay a price that day and thereafter for pain I had no part in creating. It was a sobering lesson: we may have to live with the consequences of someone else's sin even if we did not commit the sin ourselves.

As weeks went by, I wanted to be strong enough for the kids to see that our faith and trust could still lie in God and His provision even when people fail us. I tried to keep it real and let the kids feel their anger and betrayal, all while I was struggling with my own grief. I felt a slow and steady depression begin to take root. After a couple of months of just trying to maintain the structures we had in place while not getting paid, I received some surprising and welcome news from a representative of Youth Specialties (YS), a national Christian youth workers' organization. The person on the other end of the phone line said that some friends of mine back home in Oregon had nominated me for a scholarship given to one youth pastor in America to attend their annual conference—all expenses paid! I could hardly believe my ears. I felt like I was drowning and someone had just thrown me a life ring.

As I boarded the plane for California, I remember asking God what He wanted from me during this trip. I felt as if I had nothing to give. Between shame and relief, I was in awe of how God cared for me. I remember checking into the conference and saying I was the scholarship guy. This moment—and the whole YS experience— would be life changing. I began to learn that to really know the full meaning of sacrificially loving and leading others, I needed to know what it felt like to receive that kind of love and leadership from another person. "Welcome to ministry" no longer felt like drowning. This is the way of Jesus.

Over the weekend, I filled most of the available appointment times of the pastor/counselor who had made himself available to anyone hurting and needing counsel. It was as if someone had breached the Hoover Dam as I sat across from this good shepherd, this other guy named Rich. (Ironically, the leader who helped me heal had the same name as the one who harmed me.) I couldn't stop my gut-wrenching wailing. As I finally released the pain I carried, I scared myself with how much I had neatly shoved in the deep pockets of my soul. I had compartmentalized my emotions in order to carry out my responsibilities and meet everyone else's needs without being aware of my own. Seasoned as a pastor, counselor, and professor, Rich handled me with care and maturity. He listened, mirrored, validated, and empathized, even before I knew anything about those critical skills.

I was experiencing firsthand that empathy is the key factor in vulnerable leadership and healthy relationships. Dr. Brené Brown, sociologist and researcher, said in her book *Daring Greatly*, "If we can share our story with someone who responds with empathy and understanding, shame can't survive."[6] I was to learn that leaders who can slow down enough to hear those in front of them often have the smallest integrity gaps because they have let others do the same for them at some point.

I returned to Seattle with something changed in me but the same circumstances at home. I still had some fear and trepidation, but I was different. I had gained the kind of peace that surpasses all understanding (see Phil. 4:7). I didn't know what I would do or what God wanted me to do next, but I had experienced the loving presence of Jesus through the listening ear of one of His royal servants. The moment I touched down in Seattle, I walked back into the grind. Like others in the midst of gruesome circumstances, I continued to ask the Lord what He wanted me to understand and do about my situation. To be honest, I did not hear much. **I had never been that dependent on anyone in my life. That's right where the Lord wanted me.** He knew what I needed even when I had no vision for it myself.

Another month or two went by with little to no change. The peace I had experienced from the YS weekend was becoming a distant memory. Terra recalls those dark days as a season of depression for me. She sincerely reflected and prayed about whether I was the right person to be devoted to after just over a year of dating. The heaviness I carried was seeping into every aspect of my life.

In desperation, I asked to meet with our pastor and associate pastor. With my head lowered in embarrassment and burdened by defeat, I expressed that I had sincerely tried to be one of the faithful few who stayed to help them, the kids, and the community get through the fallout, but I was losing faith, hope, and love. I asked them to release me so I could go and heal. They graciously responded by affirming the call God had on my life, the heart He had given me, and the work He had allowed me to do as their youth pastor. They prayed for me and told me to stay as close as I could to a church community. As I exited the church building that day, I could feel a twelve-ton boulder being lifted off my shoulders.

When you've carried a lot of pain or been walking headlong into a steady resistance and it's suddenly removed, you notice! In Psalm 40:1–3 the psalmist perfectly communicated what I was feeling:

> I waited patiently for the LORD;
>   he turned to me and heard my cry.
> He lifted me out of the slimy pit,
>   out of the mud and mire;
> he set my feet on a rock
>   and gave me a firm place to stand.

> He put a new song in my mouth,
>> a hymn of praise to our God.
> Many will see and fear the LORD
>> and put their trust in him.

I truly felt lifted out of some heavy mud and mire, though I didn't feel like I had a clear path or a song of praise in my mouth yet. It would be years before I would see how this traumatic season of ministry would be redeemed as pain that bears new fruit.

Decades after walking out of that church building, I'm still regularly stopped in my tracks as I think through the events and relationships that God led me through during that time. With no money to keep the doors open, the church could not sustain its ministry. I often wonder where my youth-group kids are. Terra and I gave our hearts to those kids and believed God's best for them. We still do!

RED FLAGS

(Terra) After many more experiences like this one and being a therapist who works with leaders and trauma, I have grown to understand the difference between a red flag and a judgmental spirit, two signals often confused. From the very beginning, I questioned Rich's authenticity. I couldn't put my finger on why I didn't trust his words, but instead of pressing into that concern, I questioned my own integrity. Something was not right in my gut, and I often wanted to talk about it, but I felt the internal shame message that it was just me. I would pray, but the feeling would not fade.

The church teaches us to trust God and others but to always question the authenticity of our own needs or desires. This fact is important for trauma survivors to understand because abuse is a boundary crossing that teaches survivors to ignore their own feelings for the sake of a person or system. I remember knowing something was wrong yet pushing that thought or feeling (I'm not sure which was stronger) away with a louder voice: *Who tries to speak up about red flags with no proof?* This has often haunted me, as I see my own contribution to allowing harmful leaders to remain in places of power because of my own uncertainty and insecurity about rocking the boat. **If we could make room for red flags to be heard, discussed, and acted on if necessary, then the ripple effect of horrific abuse in the church would not have a place to grow.**

Since then, we have had to risk using our voices for the voiceless in hundreds of similar stories that have crossed our paths. It is common to look back and recall the signs, but in the midst of it, we are all just busy doing our jobs. Our story shines a light on the primary systemic problem the church culture faces. We must name the subtle patterns and have courage to protect the sheep from our own and others' integrity gaps. Whether you are preparing to lead or already are leading, be on mission to humbly shrink your integrity gap for the rest of your life.

Tending to our integrity gaps is a noble pursuit for all of us but especially for high-achieving leaders, who often rise to pinnacles of success to hide and feed their own agendas. Sifting through (and under) all the usual and accepted motivations that achievers have pushing them onward and upward—like an altruistic calling, passion, grit, commitment, loyalty, and discipline—there resides a deeper, hidden, and painful core motivator for most men and women at the top of their org charts.

> The church teaches us to trust God and others but to always question the authenticity of our own needs or desires.

Aspiring to leadership is a noble goal, but after two decades and thousands of hours of counseling behind closed doors with male and female achievers inside and outside the church, we've seen a concerning pattern that connects high-achieving leaders to high levels of trauma in their lives. Most leader types have had experiences where they were the caretakers, decision-makers, or wise ones in the family. Whether a child of an alcoholic where children were parentified and often tried to keep the alcoholic happy, or the oldest in a workaholic home where siblings were left to figure out life on their own, learning to navigate stressful environments serves well for a time, until the external stressors outgrow the body's capacity. As leaders are propelled by an ability to outperform their peers, unresolved trauma shapes and influences the lives of both leaders and those in their leadership wake until the leaders can no longer keep their stories hidden.

This largely unknown connection (though vaguely felt at some level) between leaders and trauma is real. For high-level leaders, hiding behind achievements and successes insulates them from addressing the trauma that got them achieving in the first place. Since **charisma**

and capacity outrank character in today's culture, we are setting ourselves up for widespread havoc. Not all leaders have unresolved trauma. And not all leaders have large integrity gaps. In fact, most of us are in the middle realm, where our short tempers, Netflix binges, and lack of boundaries seem normal. We smile and think, *At least* …[7]

THE CALL

The role of leadership is socially acceptable and creates coping strategies for leaders to run and hide from their unresolved trauma. **As long as leaders remain in power, retain control, and are viewed as necessary, no one seems to look closer to notice how they may be hiding, hurting, or repeating abuse within their carefully guarded and managed systems of influence.** Sometimes living from our own integrity means we must step out of systems that bring only damage, not life, no matter how much long-suffering we're ready to bear. In fact, sometimes staying in these systems enables unhealthy functioning rather than creating change.

Some of the most influential leaders are those who face their integrity gaps with honesty and courage and allow their followers to grieve and share with them. In our experience, this has looked like a seasoned couple during their empty-nest years finally being able to recognize how their childhoods affected their marriage. Wishing they had started earlier, they find healing for their marriage by doing the hard work of facing their long-unmet needs and doing repair work with their adult children. Incredible!

If you're reading this book and identify yourself as a Christian, will you join us in this mission of first shrinking your own gap (a lifelong endeavor) and then helping others shrink theirs? It might sound obvious, but you don't want to reverse the order! We are calling leaders from a position of grace, not from a position of judgment. As we all know, the world doesn't need any more judgmental Christians. If you're reading this book and do not identify yourself as a Christian, will you also join us in the quest to shrink our integrity gaps and help others do the same? It hurts to be in the wake of a leader who does not care or is unaware that his or her own pain is leaking in destructive ways. We think we can all agree that smaller integrity gaps mean good for the human race.

By now, we hope we have made the case for a higher quality of leadership at every level, especially among those of us who consider ourselves followers of Jesus Christ. This can happen only as leaders everywhere and at every level work to shrink their gaps with humility as they experience real grace. It's from this authentic position that they are able to help others do likewise with credibility. Whether you're a single parent working three jobs or you're at the top of the org chart ensuring your people have quality healthcare, how you live and lead matters! If you are a leader of many, you have the privilege of inspiring, influencing, and supporting many. Who knows? Your actions might motivate a child or a young adult to explore politics, enter Christian ministry, start a business, or join a nonprofit that literally changes the world!

The younger generation in your leadership wake is already watching, learning, and vowing either to be like you or to be different. Millennials are the largest adult generation in the US (they'll compose more than 75 percent of the labor force by 2025). This generation and the generation following them (like our daughters) "need leaders who set [them] up for success, instill in [them] a sense of bigger purpose, and give [them] the confidence [they] need to persevere when the work gets challenging."[8] Like Paul, who said, "Follow my example, as I follow the example of Christ" (1 Cor. 11:1), give them as many reasons as possible to want to be like you.

As they hide to cope with their past trauma, leaders often perpetuate trauma in their spheres of influence.

Now that we've laid the foundation, we will take the remaining nine chapters to unpack the symptoms that can take achievers and leaders into hiding places where their gaps often increase. As they hide to cope with their past trauma, leaders often perpetuate trauma in their spheres of influence. It is our intention to not only clarify the problems but to also identify specific antidotes for each symptom, either to keep you from falling into these common and subtle traps or to help you get out if you're open to a leg up. Although these symptoms are not an exhaustive list, we've seen them in leaders during more than four decades of living and two decades of private practice, executive coaching, and organizational development. If you are an achiever/leader type, realize you are at risk, but don't let this warning lead you to fear or quit. Stay humble, root yourself in the grace you have received, and commit to becoming the leader you would follow. Really lead.

Antidotes

1. Name those you influence (consider your marriage, family, work, neighborhood, community, school, etc.) and how they might be affected by the gap in your integrity.

2. Make a list of leaders you personally know and respect. What characteristics do they exemplify? How do you know they are people of integrity?

3. Make a list of leaders who have harmed you or whom you have seen struggle in their leadership. Name some of the warning signs you saw along the way. What do you know about their recovery process?

4. CHALLENGE: Ask three of the people closest to you where they see you living with integrity and where they see you having a gap. Receive this as a starting point in your journey toward becoming a healthy and Wholehearted Leader.

Part II

SYMPTOMS OF INTEGRITY GAPS

Chapter 3

TRAUMA AND TRIGGERS

The Past Is Not in the Past

The past is never where you think you left it.
—Katherine Anne Porter, *Ship of Fools*

Even though you cannot change the events of your story,
you can change the way you experience your story.
—Curt Thompson, *Anatomy of the Soul*

Most of us go through our days checking off our to-do lists, doing things for God, and achieving our goals. We get mad. We get sad. We surely get frustrated in the middle of rush-hour traffic. But few of us stop to consider that what we are experiencing in the very present—*an unhappy marriage, a short temper with our kids, loss of enjoyment in our work*—could be more related to our past than what we are currently enduring. Let's explore.

JEFF'S STORY

(Jeff) Have you ever felt an overwhelming surge of negative emotion (uncontrollable rage, debilitating fear, or an overpowering urge to flee) when there was no logical reason in the moment for the intense emotion? This is called a trigger. A <u>trigger is an intense emotional</u> or <u>physical reaction to anything the mind associates with a past trauma.</u> Most of the time, these triggers are subconscious and it takes intentionality to uncover their roots.

Terra and I had been married for six years before our first daughter, Addie, arrived. I never knew I could love anyone *so much*! At the time Terra had just started her private practice. Addie was only a few months old, and on the days Terra was in session, I stepped away from my work as the children's pastor at our church to be with Addie. What a gift to experience this time with my little girl. But I'll never forget the day something snapped inside me.

Everything was going great until Addie started getting a little fussy. No problem. With my list of baby strategies (feeding, napping, changing, soothing, playing), I just had to figure out what she needed. Nothing was working, and "a little fussy" turned into full-on screaming! Although not a first, this was rare for Addie. I mentally assessed my list again. *What is going on?*

I felt helpless as her screams blasted me in the face, and that's when I felt it. Though I was not aware at the time, my brain was literally shifting as blood left my frontal lobe (the reasoning part of my brain) and rushed to my amygdala (the part of my brain responsible for fight, flight, or freeze) to activate a reaction in response to what was perceived as "danger." I realized that part of me was losing perspective. Instead of using the calm, gentle tone she had always previously heard from me, I remember yelling, "Why is this happening?" and "Why won't you stop screaming? I'm trying to help you!" In the heat of the moment, I thought of her more as an "it" than as my baby daughter, whom I love with my whole heart. (Please know that our daughter was not harmed.)

All my muscles were tensed up, and I believe God then suddenly intervened in my heart and mind, as if He were standing next to me while I held my little girl. I listened to the still small voice and knew I needed to put her down. Thankfully, I submitted to God's wisdom and help in that moment.

I settled Addie back in her crib (screams and all), shut the door, and dropped to the floor to do as many push-ups as I could to relax. I had never been so terrified in my life! I was flooded with a mix of shame, remorse, and gratitude that I was coming back to who I want to be. *What just happened? How could I be so mad at my little girl? Nothing was her fault! What is your problem, Jeff? This isn't something you're going to be able to figure out on your own.* I made a commitment right then to connect with a counselor. After reaching near-total exhaustion from the push-ups, I stood up, went back into Addie's nursery, and picked up my still-screaming daughter to comfort her. As I held her and sang our favorite song, she eventually calmed down.

Between the moment I came face to face with my hidden rage and the moment I walked through the door of my counselor's office, I had been trying to figure out what was wrong with me. All my adult life I had wanted to be a dad, but suddenly I was questioning my own parenting. It would take a few sessions to get there, but with my counselor it became clear: my inability to control my screaming child was a trigger event that catapulted me back to a traumatic incident I witnessed as a boy. The connection to my own past hit me hard.

In my early-elementary years (close to the age of seven), I woke up to the sound of a tomcat hissing and screaming in our backyard. The next thing I remember, I saw my dad running out back in his nightclothes, carrying my baseball bat. And then—*whack!* The cat was dead. I was scared and quickly ducked down so my dad couldn't see me watching from my second-story bedroom window, but I heard and saw the whole thing as clearly as a movie. I heard my dad reenter the house and return to his bedroom across the hall from the room my little brother and I shared. I glanced at my brother, and fortunately, he was fast asleep. The fear of the experience had me up for hours, and at the same time, I was thinking, *Wow! My dad is powerful! He took that stupid, whiny cat and solved that problem.*

Now I have come to understand, from both my own story and the stories of most abuse survivors, that it is common to experience the dichotomy of feeling terror at the same time as you align yourself with the person in power, like a parent. This kind of internal conflict is called ambivalence—we find ourselves divided between love and hate, fear and awe, need and avoidance. We straddle this indecision because if we decide a person or an event is "bad," then we are unsure if we can outlive the cost. Dan Allender, the author of *The Wounded Heart*, discussed ambivalence as "a profound and normal experience in life, especially for those who are in the middle of living out significant desire in the face of deep uncertainty, and with a history of significant harm."[1]

I remember that the next morning I woke up wondering, *What did my dad do with the dead cat?* Summoning all my courage, I went outside and looked around the backyard. With my small hands trembling and my heart ready to leap out of my chest (I still get chills at the thought of this moment, and I'm in my forties!), I opened the trash can lid and saw the carcass. I slammed the lid shut and ran away! Several months later, I woke up to the sound of another whiny cat and my dad leaving his bedroom. This time I jumped out of bed and intercepted him in the hallway. "Dad, can I help?" My fear was soon replaced with a rush of adrenaline and delight as my dad allowed me to join him. (Now as an adult and parent, this saddens me on so many levels even though I now better understand abusive systems.)

At first I felt victorious as my dad silenced another stray cat. I tried to act tough, but then after I went inside, washed my hands, and tucked myself back into bed, I cried my eyes out because of what I had done. My own conscience (the Spirit of God inside me) battled with my desire to be like my dad. I knew I didn't want to help like that anymore. After that night, I wished for no cat to ever enter our property again. This particular type of abuse was only the tip of the iceberg of my own experiences, and I would later discover more within our entire family system. Ambivalence became a familiar experience throughout my growing years.

A deep-seated fear of repeating the abusive behavior that I and other members of my family survived was what drove me to get the help I needed. In my counseling, working with an experienced trauma-informed clinician, I learned that the feelings I had struggled with as I held my baby girl were somehow connected to the trauma of witnessing my dad kill those two cats. It was hard to believe that these two events separated by more than twenty-five years were intertwined, but my past was dramatically affecting my present. If I had hidden my past or denied its impact, it definitely could have affected my future! I shudder to think of what eventually could have happened or what I would have become over time. I sense the power of God's grace in my life as I consider the possibilities now.

This gigantic aha from counseling signified a moment when I became aware of my own integrity gap. My gap existed because of the distance between the values I espoused (what I said I was about) and the values I actually lived out. I know I loved my baby daughter, and I would have readily given my life to save hers. Yet, as I have now learned, not being able to solve the problem of her screaming was the trigger that got me in touch with the trauma I had experienced all those years ago with my dad and the cats. I thank God for intervening that day with Addie.

I began to shrink my gap after my counselor helped me process the first trauma and then gave me new skills I could use when interacting with my daughter. If I ever felt that crazy surge again, I would be equipped to interrupt the moment and regulate it in a healthy way for us both. **Dragging my fear and that scary experience into the light was one of the most important things I could have ever done.** As a result, Terra and I were on the same page, and with lots of practice, that intense reaction eventually went away. New experiences that reinforce God's DNA in our lives can heal old wounds locked up in our neuropathways, giving us a new ability to trust who God says we are regardless of our stories and behaviors.

UNDERSTANDING TRIGGERS

I realize that what I just shared was a lot for some of you (probably most of you). Rest assured that my daughter was not abused in any way. Getting help with what I was feeling (and couldn't yet understand) was the key to preventing anything from occurring in the future. I'm not sharing this story to lead you to some grandiose perception of me. That kind of thinking must end in order for me to break away from the culture of abuse and narcissism that I grew up in.

> Burying unresolved trouble won't keep it hidden. Unaddressed guilt, shame, and other feelings leak into our lives (whether we're aware of it or not).

As we mentioned earlier, a trigger is an internal response to an external stimulus that the brain associates with a past experience, ultimately influencing an external behavior. Maybe you have felt a reaction jump out of nowhere and it scared you to death. Maybe you have felt a slow and steady build over time and have forgotten what peace or normal feels like in your body. Maybe you have found yourself reacting in ways that seem far from who you or who others know you to be. Wanting to hide things that scare or embarrass us is a normal reaction but a dangerous one. Burying unresolved trouble won't keep it hidden. Unaddressed guilt, shame, and other feelings leak into our lives (whether we're aware of it or not). The longer we attempt to hide or run from these feelings and experiences, the more likely we are to compartmentalize our lives in a way that increases our integrity gaps and the inevitable consequences.

(Terra) As Jeff's wife and mama bear to our two precious girls, I was so grateful for Jeff's honesty and willingness to do his own work at that time in our lives. In our six years together prior to having children, I had never seen this kind of trauma response from him. Jeff already wanted to build a different legacy from his original family's, but all we knew about the story of his family of origin was what he had been able to process and the narratives his family told over time. Now he had a counselor wife who thought she knew how to prevent every dysfunction in the book. (A little humility, life, and maturity have been good teachers for this therapist!) As two type-A, oldest, achiever children, if we could have conquered this trauma in our premarital counseling six years earlier, you bet we would have!

What Jeff was experiencing as a new dad with a crying baby was normal. However, for someone with unresolved triggers, like an abuse survivor, it's harder to discern and regulate responses to normal life circumstances. **Trauma gets stored in the emotional brain—which is not logical—and produces involuntary physical responses to perceived danger.** The brain can jump from a logical thought like *I feel angry, and I need to calm down* to *I feel angry, and I need to fight, fly, or freeze* in just a matter of seconds. Though the current people, circumstances, and environments may be different, the brain categorizes experiences along familiar neuropathways. The trouble occurs when the body confuses a safe experience with an unsafe one. Learning how to slow down this automatic response takes awareness and practice.

Some triggers hide in compartmentalized parts of our brains as a God-given protection to get us through the tragedy of our stories. In a way, we see this as part of God's grace in designing us in such a way to help us navigate pain. In fact, the more trauma one experiences, the more fragmented and compartmentalized one becomes. This response is due to the nature of living in a fallen world and finding a clever coping strategy that helps us survive. When we are in the midst of a literal or figurative war, we are not able to process meaning or make sense of what we see. Without human comfort, coaching, processing, redeeming experiences, or a compass to point the way toward healing, we use clever coping to make sense of life, our identity, God, and our relationships that are a bit askew. We have to remember that "grace is not soft on sin. Attempting to manage my sin is."[2]

TRAUMA IN LEADERS

Trauma survivors can change the world when their tolerance for difficulties and ability to survive the worst situations are channeled in the right direction—a God-oriented direction. The most radical and courageous leaders are the ones who have vulnerably connected the dots within their stories: processing, grieving, and finally accepting the outcomes. In contrast, the worst kind of leaders are the ones who are least integrated—most compartmentalized—in how they move through their lives, completely unaware of how they affect themselves and others. Whether we admit it or not, our stories matter. God designed us to bring all of who we are to Him and to others so we can experience the closure and healing that will allow us to live with peace in the present and with hope for the future. In his profound book *Anatomy of the Soul,* Curt Thompson said, "To love God with all of our mind is to engage our entire memory, not limited parts of it.... It is about remembering our past and anticipating our future. It is about a God who will not be kept at a distance but uses each of our stories to confront, terrify, comfort, convict, and woo us…. Your memory creates your future. That's because you imagine the future through the neural networks created by your past."[3]

> The most radical and courageous leaders are the ones who have vulnerably connected the dots within their stories: processing, grieving, and finally accepting the outcomes.

Returning to the analogy from chapter 2 of the car in park, flooring the gas pedal eventually breaks down the engine. Too often we resort to managing our sin, trying to white-knuckle our way through difficult circumstances without ever assessing why our foot is on the gas pedal in the first place. Thompson reminds us, "One way to comprehend the dynamic of sin is to see it as a matter of choosing to be mindless rather than mindful, which ultimately leads to our minds becoming dis-integrated."[4] In other words, becoming more aware of our unique stories and neurobiology leads us to be more integrated, moving us toward digging up the roots of our sin patterns instead of just plucking weeds.

Many of us find clever ways to cope and have learned how to hide our trauma well. In her book *Strengthening the Soul of Your Leadership*, Ruth Haley Barton related a conversation between Theophane, a Cistercian monk, and another monk.

Theophane asked, "Brother, what is your dream?"

He replied, "I would like to become a monk."

Theophane said, "But brother, you are a monk, aren't you?"

As he revealed a gun under his robe, the monk replied, "I've been here for 25 years, but I still carry a gun."

"Why don't you give it up?" asked Theophane.

The monk replied, "I guess I've had it so long. I've been hurt a lot, and I've hurt a lot of others. I don't think I would be comfortable without this gun."

Theophane said, "But you seem pretty uncomfortable with it."[5]

Barton went on to say, "Most of us have a gun—some way of protecting ourselves and making ourselves feel safe, hidden under the robe of our leadership persona. It is fairly easy to keep our gun hidden most of the time, but *we* know that it is there and that it is incongruent with the person God is calling us to be."[6] It is typical to keep our "guns" for when we feel out of control. Similar to the monk's gun, Jeff's quickly rising rage was a way to protect himself. Becoming a new father presented an opportunity to learn a new way.

Barton continued, "Learning to pay attention and knowing what to pay attention *to* is a key discipline for leaders but one that rarely comes naturally to those of us who are barreling through life with our eyes fixed on a goal.... If we take time to pay attention, we see that God was with us."[7] It is by God's grace that we ever feel ready to hand over our protection mechanisms. For Jeff, it was a matter of choosing harming those he loved most and submitting himself to a process of becoming more integrated and whole, laying down the figurative gun. Every great leader of integrity comes face to face with these moments. The question is whether we are paying attention to the sirens blaring in our bodies, our relationships, and our souls.

Barton explored the life of Moses and how he had to reconcile his past before he could continue in his leadership.[8] Moses had been abandoned two times by his own mother and adopted by an Egyptian princess, and he was working through being Jewish yet having been raised by his people's oppressors. He must have felt extreme ambivalence, as both sides were his family. Rage must have built over time as his survivor's guilt became too much to bear. Moses was having an identity crisis, and the climax came when he killed a man. **His coping strategies had served him well in the past but were no longer appropriate for the leader he needed to become.** Before he could lead the people of Israel into freedom, Moses needed to experience his own freedom through healing.

Key Markers of Trauma and Triggers

- Your responses to the world are perceived as overreacting and hypervigilance.
- You feel numb and void of appropriate feelings (flat affect).
- You find yourself constantly self-shaming and feeling angry or irritable.
- You experience unresolved depression or anxiety.
- You feel emotionally disconnected from your story, rarely remembering your childhood or important events in your recent life.

- You're often unable to calm your body down (consciously or unconsciously), so use unhealthy means to reduce stress and anxiety.

Antidotes

Sometimes the only way to face our present and past is with the skilled help of a trained guide. Counselors cannot do the "hike" for you, but they know the trails well and can tell you when you've reached the top. You get to take the hike at your own pace but with a guide who can keep you accountable for pacing yourself and finishing well. A counselor's trained expertise and boundaries will allow you to sort through what is yours to own and what is yours to heal from. He or she will also help you take steps toward reconciling your current living with the life you want to lead.

1. Find a trusted and respected mental health professional who can help you unpack your story and any hidden part of your life in a confidential setting. Good counselors (both from a character and competency standpoint) should be willing to hold themselves to the highest standard of accountability and ethics. This translates into a both/and approach: holding a biblical worldview and ethic as well as voluntarily submitting to the field's standards in order to do no harm. Similar to searching for a heart surgeon, invest the time. Find a quality Christian mental health professional who has training and up-to-date credentials, either licensed or pursuing licensure under supervisors of character and competence. Look into this person's reputation, and learn what to expect from professionals according to the

laws of your state. Counselors integrating these standards into their lives and practice offer higher-quality care to their clients, as they are shrinking their own personal and professional integrity gaps. If you are not ready for a counselor, try a spiritual director or life coach to begin.

2. Write out a family genogram (see appendix A for a sample). This is a powerful tool to reveal the patterns in your family system and bring awareness to the behaviors that were modeled in it.

3. Write out a time line of your life from birth to present day. This may include stories you have been told and actual memories. If you recall it, it's important, so write it down. Then identify the lessons you have learned from your story. Your memories will tell how you understand yourself, God, and relationships.

4. Try journaling. The mere practice of writing down what's in your mind, heart, and body is proven not only to heal the soul but also to reduce stress and increase awareness.

5. Read some of the books we referenced in this chapter. Each of them will help you in your journey toward becoming a Wholehearted Leader.

6. If you have past trauma or think your present addictions and mal-adaptive coping strategies are severe, find someone who is a trauma therapist and does EMDR (eye movement desensitization and re-processing). EMDR is a clinically proven treatment for mind, heart,

body, and spirit integration work. Since trauma is stored in the body, this powerful tool helps the body catch up to where the mind, heart, and spirit want to go. At Living Wholehearted, all our clinicians consistently use EMDR as a way to help connect the dots between the past and present. The benefits:

- allows us to grieve unknown areas of our past and helps the emotional brain tell its story without rationalizing away feelings
- reduces triggers and unwanted reactions and behaviors by desensitizing us from the effects of trauma
- helps untold numbers of military veterans and first responders deal with PTSD-like symptoms

Chapter 4

GUILT AND TOXIC SHAME

If They Only Knew

Shame makes us want to hide ourselves. It makes us feel like we have a dark side that no one sees, and we believe that no one would love us if they knew the truth.

—Tristen and Jonathan Collins, *Why Emotions Matter*

Hiding trauma or their response to it will cause leaders to live with an immense amount of guilt and shame. You may think you have successfully kept things neatly tucked in your past, at least well enough to keep on keeping on, but they're leaking into your present, whether you're aware of it or not. You might even think things are "just fine," a subtle lie we hold tight to in order to keep from unraveling. The very fact that you are reading this book might be the cue for you to get help—for yourself, for those you say you love, and for the lives in your leadership wake.

Regardless of our stories, shame seems to find its way into the crevices of our lives. Tristen and Jonathan Collins have said, "Shame is a type of disgust that only humans appear to be capable of: disgust with ourselves. It's a gut reaction that tells us *we are gross*, that we should be avoided by others."[1] It's really at the root of so many of our unhealthy systems. It can be a quiet voice or one that shades our entire existence. However, sometimes we confuse shame with the guilt we feel over our hidden lives. Shame and guilt are two completely different things. Shame is one of Satan's greatest weapons to attack our identity and tear down God's most treasured creation—us. Instead of the voice that says, *That was a bad choice I made. What do I need to do to correct it?*, shame sounds like *You are bad, and you'll never learn.* The apostle John, who walked with Jesus and witnessed the unlimited power of God over the limited power of Satan, recorded what Jesus had to say about the Evil One: "The thief comes only to steal and kill and destroy; I came that they may have life, and have it abundantly" (John 10:10 NASB).

Shame is the result of experiencing our sin or the sin done to us, and Satan uses shame to deepen the pain of our wounds and to attack our identity. This has been the dance since Genesis.

Guilt is tied to our engagement in behavior that is contrary to God's will for our lives. We feel guilt because of our behavior, not our personhood. If we do not experience guilt, we lack consciences and empathy, becoming numb to the effects of hurtful choices. In this way, guilt is a gift. Feelings of guilt alert us that we're thinking or acting outside of God's best for our lives. God provides us with the uneasy sense of guilt—the Holy Spirit inside followers of Jesus—to correct our courses back to our originally intended design. Attuned leaders see this guidance as a gift to help them live congruently with who they are made to be.

For those secure in Jesus Christ, we have the Holy Spirit in us (God in us 24-7 … imagine it!). The Spirit's primary function in Christians' lives is to remind them of all Jesus has taught through

Scripture, prayer, and their communities of faith (see John 14:26). As we read and apply God's Word to our lives on a regular basis, the Holy Spirit can help us access these resources we store in our hearts and minds at each turn. Galatians 5 speaks of the importance of staying in step with the Spirit: "My counsel is this: Live freely, animated and motivated by God's Spirit. Then you won't feed the compulsions of selfishness" (v. 16 THE MESSAGE). The Spirit reminds us of who God says He is and who God says we are and saves us from the darker tendencies we all have. Staying in step with the Spirit is not about trying harder but rather submitting ourselves to a different voice. The voice of grace points to our identity as chosen, loved, known, and significant, apart from what we do. The voice of shame urges us toward the never-ending treadmill of trying to prove we are worthy.

SAM'S STORY

We met our friend Sam, the founding pastor of a large church, through a leadership cohort. After more than twenty years of colaboring, Sam went to his friends and the elders of the church to tell them about his integrity gap. He disclosed that he had been struggling with a porn addiction and needed help. We'll never forget hearing Sam share about the resulting tragic experience he and his family had been enduring in the years since.

Sam responded to the Holy Spirit's nudge to come clean about his hidden sex addiction. He could see how it was hurting God, himself, his family, and those he shepherded. Sam was compelled to confess, to begin the process of turning from his harmful ways, and to seek professional counseling. Even though he was ready for help, his friends and the elders of the church were processing their own pain and were not able or ready to help. In fact, the church leaders subjected him (and, consequently, his wife and kids) to a tainted and humiliating narrative: from the pulpit and in formal and informal communications within the church and their community. Sam described the further shaming caused by church leaders who were his friends, colleagues, and co-ministers of the gospel as "devastating." Their treatment of him hijacked his healing (and their healing) and reinforced Sam's internal narrative: *I am bad and broken beyond repair.*

When a leader initiates a confession of a hidden behavior or addiction, the situation is rarely handled with care and wisdom. The mass explosion of everyone's shame interferes with God's redemptive process. This breaks our hearts. We are not saying that a healthy response happens without damage to all parties involved. In fact, the shock and betrayal are real and can take time to unpack. Shame begets shame, and as we will discuss further, while owning consequences is part of the healing, *owning shame is not.* Learning to slow down to disentangle shame from guilt is vital whether we are the one disclosing or the one betrayed.

Forgiveness often requires us to wrestle with "how our righteous God is both merciful *and* faithful to meet the evils of this world with a right response."

Scripture speaks about how to handle those who have contrite hearts and those who do not. (We will continue to unpack the latter in the following chapters.) In 2 Corinthians 2 we read about Paul's experience of confronting the church. Though we are uncertain what the offense was, Paul had been deeply grieved by someone's sin but now said, "The punishment inflicted on him [the offending party] by the majority is sufficient. Now instead, you ought to forgive and comfort him, so that he will not be overwhelmed by excessive sorrow [shame]. I urge you, therefore, to reaffirm your love for him" (vv. 6–8). We know the process of forgiveness requires time and intentionality from all parties involved. It's important to mention that forgiveness does not equal trust but is an important ingredient for moving toward any form of closure. One biblical word often translated "forgive" literally means "to let go," indicating that we should name the origins of the offense, acknowledge the cost and full impact, and then let God be in charge of the outcomes. Forgiveness often requires us to wrestle with "how our righteous God is both merciful *and* faithful to meet the evils of this world with a right response."[2]

Despite it all, Sam grasped what might have happened if he had hidden his sex addiction any longer and was ready to make things right with his God and those he loved. Though his community was unable to move toward him when he confessed, he chose to do the necessary work to heal, which led him to grieve his past. Many addicts, especially sex addicts, share a common trait of not knowing how to move toward others, process difficult emotions, or receive comfort in intimate relationships.[3] As a child, Sam had learned to receive love in his home through performance, and he constantly longed for the approval of his parents. When his father left the family for another woman, he started coping with this stress through pornography. The common fear of being discovered and drowning in shame (disgust with himself) kept Sam hiding longer than he ever wanted. Sam was convinced that God would remove His hand of blessing from him, similar to what he read about God doing with a famous biblical leader, King Saul.

IN THE BIBLE

Many lessons can be pulled from the stories of King Saul and King David, their clearly different heart responses to sin, and the outcomes of their lives. Saul became the first anointed king of Israel because the Israelites clamored for a king like other nations. They persisted in their desire for a person they could look to as their champion—an idol of sorts. God reluctantly gave them their wish—but also the consequences of placing someone in God's rightful place. Saul received God's blessing and favor, but as time went on, he relied more on himself and directly disobeyed God's instructions. Rather than grieving over his sin, Saul desperately tried to control his narrative and others' perception of him. He was unwilling to accept the cost of his choices and shed pseudorepentant tears over being caught —but then continued to manipulate outcomes. Saul was not well in his mind or heart after years of leading in his own strength while pretending to be dependent on God. Because Saul refused grace, God removed His blessing from him and raised up another leader, David (see 1 Sam. 8–31).

King David knew the reality of having it all (a heart after God, anointed power, wealth, and influence) and then crashing. David lusted, committed adultery, and then covered up a murder. David continued praising and worshipping God in public while hiding the treachery he had been committing. Because God loved David, He pursued him. When God's prophet, Nathan, confronted him to bring his sin into the light, David did what he had done a thousand times—he humbled himself before almighty God (see 2 Sam. 11–12). David's psalms display this authentic humility. Particularly in Psalm 51, we see his brokenness, his confession, his submission, and his cries for mercy and for the restoration of his relationship with God.

> Create in me a pure heart, O God,
>> and renew a steadfast spirit within me.
> Do not cast me from your presence
>> or take your Holy Spirit from me.
> Restore to me the joy of your salvation
>> and grant me a willing spirit, to sustain me.
>> (vv. 10–12)

Although God forgave David and loved him and Bathsheba, He did not withhold the consequences of sin. The baby conceived in their lust was born but became ill and died, as God had said it would. God continued to love and bless David for many more years, but the systemic effects of his choices reached into the next generation (see 2 Sam. 12–19).

In *A Tale of Three Kings*, Gene Edwards contrasted the men and their responses when confronted with their sin: "In God's sacred school of submission and brokenness, why are there so few students?

Because all who are in this school must suffer much pain. And as you might guess, it is often the unbroken ruler (whom God sovereignly picks) who metes out the pain. David was once a student in this school, and Saul was God's chosen way to crush David."[4] God foreknew that David, a man whom He considered to have a heart bent toward Him (see 1 Sam. 13:14), would fall into sin. God knew that David would need brutal refinement to intimately understand His love, His protection, His provision, and His grace.

After confessing his addiction, Sam faced his greatest moments of vulnerability, like David, craving God's grace and presence in the darkest days of his and his family's lives. Even though their church family and communities exhibited normal levels of shock, they did not give any consideration to whether Sam had a heart like Saul or like David as they reacted to the news. Unfortunately, it is typical for churches to respond by either helping leaders hide or by kicking them while they are down, both responses to systemic shame. Referencing Barton's story, when someone openly hands you his metaphorical gun used for protection and sincerely says he is ready to give it up, don't shoot him with it.

SHRINKING THIS GAP

In order for leaders to honestly face their past (and hand over their guns), we need to close the integrity gap that exists in our churches and Christian organizations. We say we believe that God forgives sinners and is the answer to our addictions, our pain, and our brokenness, but then we withhold grace-filled responses from Christian leaders (who are men and women just like the rest of us) when they come forward in confession and repentance, seeking help and healing. **Once leaders taste the peace that comes from trusting God and others to protect them, rather than relying on their own maladaptive coping strategies, they experience God's provision for themselves and their loved ones.** This changes leaders and accomplishes work only God can do!

Though letting God and others into the crevices of our lives takes enormous courage, this is what it means to give our whole hearts to Jesus. Curt Thompson said,

> To be known is to be pursued, examined, and shaken. To be known is to be loved and to have hopes and even demands placed on you. It is to risk, not only the furniture in your home being rearranged, but your floor plans being rewritten, your walls being demolished and reconstructed. To be known means that you allow your shame and guilt to be exposed— in order for them to be healed....
>
> Christianity is not about being right. It's about being loved.[5]

The longer we hide, the more devastating the consequences. Submitting to the provision of God and others—through confession and repentance—often doesn't remove the practical consequences of our decision to sin. It does, however, bring about an internal peace with God that cannot be overvalued. When we bring what is hidden into the light and find we are still loved, shame has no oxygen to survive. Having peace with God and ourselves is the most important and wonderful reality we can ever experience in this life!

The wholehearted life—a life that is integrated and aware—is what all people are searching for whether they call themselves Christian or not. It offers the kind of peace that sustained the believers in the Coliseum when they were fed to the lions. It offers the kind of peace that fed the faith of Cassie Bernall, the seventeen-year-old girl who was executed in the 1999 Columbine High School massacre for professing that she believed in God. It offers the kind of conviction and peace that allowed Abraham Lincoln to endure the visceral hatred aimed at him for the immense loss and staggering casualties of the Civil War.

Maintaining the same kind of peace requires conviction. It may lead you to reject lucrative business ventures that would surely compromise your integrity and faith. You may need to come clean about the way you took advantage of others, harming them intentionally or unintentionally. No matter what the sin or the scope of its consequences, the grace, forgiveness, and peace God brings are far greater.

> When we bring what is hidden into the light and find we are still loved, shame has no oxygen to survive.

We need God's peace, but we don't get it on our terms. He directs us to repent and confess to another as the only way to start to resolve guilt, reshape our neuropathways, and crush the toxic shame we feel. James 5:16 says, "Confess your sins to each other and pray for each other so that you may be healed." The experience of confessing to another human being and being heard, comforted, and prayed for brings healing. Neuropsychology reminds us that new ways of thinking and being (neuropathways) only change when we have new and consistent experiences. This is often why believers will say they know they are forgiven but do not feel or act like they are forgiven. Barton once said, "One thing we can know for sure is that when we are confessing our sin to God but not to the people around us in ordinary, nitty-gritty life, there is not much real spiritual transformation going on."[6] Healing includes repairing relationships with those we have harmed when it is time. New experiences over a consistent period of time create new narratives, replacing the lies that once fueled the harmful coping strategies we used to hide our shame.

Many never consider that a traumatic childhood experience and shame could get stuck in the body and suddenly reemerge decades later in a seemingly unrelated way. Yet our past cultural norms, church experiences, families of origin, and trauma are behind the door of every present-day choice we make ... unless we take time to unravel the impact of emotions and beliefs and unlearn some of the coping strategies we were never meant to rely on. In the deepest part of who we are, we are made to be led to freedom as we submit ourselves to God and His way of grace and redemption. Even if you face consequences for things you've done as a result of deep unmet needs and past pain, you can have His approval, His love, His protection, His peace. This is amazing news.

We are inviting you into this journey too. We know we bring nothing but our brokenness to the table, but we also believe in who God says He is and who He says we are: loved, resilient, and significant—regardless of our past stories and present circumstances. Because we've been shown grace, mercy, and forgiveness, we are

learning to do likewise for those within our influence. There is nothing like it. This is God within us and working through each of us.

Key Markers of Guilt and Toxic Shame

- You live from a place of "should," or you confuse doing something wrong with being bad.
- You need people to see how "good" you are because you are
not sure your identity is secure in what God says.
- You fear that disappointing God or others will cause you to be
abandoned.
- You have a hard time owning when you do something wrong
because you think it means you are owning that something is
wrong with you.
- You use defensiveness, blaming, judgmentalism, self-depreca-
tion, and stonewalling to hide feelings of shame.
- You find it difficult to separate what you do from who you are.

Antidotes

1. If you have already invested in counseling and are aware of your
story but need someone outside your system to help you process, remain grounded in health, and avoid hiding parts of your life, consider
meeting weekly with one or two friends for honest conversations.

2. Ask three people you trust to give you feedback about whether
they see any harmful patterns or other concerns in your life. When
you are ready to hear from those you care about (your spouse,

children, closest friends, pastor), it's a good sign you have a heart like David's. The hardest part then becomes implementing the feedback.

3. Ask three to five people to write down who they see you to be. These affirmations will help you see beyond your shame. Put these words in a place where you will see them daily to help you discern the difference between your personhood and your actions.

4. For the repentant heart:
- Make a list of those you have harmed (intentionally and unintentionally).
- Prayerfully consider how your actions affected each person and how each might feel.
- With counsel, consider how you might make amends.
- Thank God for His forgiveness, and trust Him to help those still hurting.

5. For the offended:
- Make a list of what actions and behaviors have harmed you.
- Prayerfully consider how those actions affected you and made you feel.
- With counsel, consider how you might extend forgiveness and make amends.

Chapter 5

ESCAPISM AND COMPARTMENTALIZATION

Everybody Loves Me … Outside My House

A house doesn't make a home.
—U2, "Sometimes You Can't Make It on Your Own"

A jack pine "solitary on its rocky point" is one of the loveliest sights I know. But lovelier still is the sight of a man or woman standing with integrity intact.… You catch a glimpse of the beauty that arises when people refuse to live divided lives.
—Parker Palmer, *A Hidden Wholeness*

A toxic infection started in the homes of leaders many generations ago, and it has gone largely untreated, even as it has exacted a tremendous cost from families. In home after home, fathers and mothers who go to work do so to escape. What are they escaping from? Many are going to great lengths to escape things that don't make them feel good at home. They may be happy to have a reprieve of eight to fourteen (or more) hours from marriage concerns, the unending hardships of raising kids, and the turmoil of their internal world. Home has become something to endure or—worse—a place

97

to pretend in while they develop a secret life they think no one will ever discover if they control things well enough. The escape-mentality infection and its associated behaviors are actually symptoms of a much deeper lie rooted in pain but easily believed.

THE LIE

We have been taught that we deserve to be successful and happy and that it's possible to control the various spheres of our lives to produce maximum happiness. Because this is a lie, it can be achieved only in part by compartmentalizing your life in an effort to protect your heart from pain. *Compartmentalization* can be defined as "the division of something into sections or categories."[1] On the other end of the spectrum, living wholehearted means that we do not live divided but rather bring all the parts of who we are to every relationship and task before us. Though learned through family systems, unhealthy compartmentalizing becomes a clever coping strategy to keep from ever feeling or being fully known, and it leads to far greater consequences than people realize. In other words, it acts as a false protection of our hearts and feeds another lie—that we are not valuable. It causes us to lose sight of those who matter most and instead make everything about "me, myself, and I."

> Living wholehearted means that we do not live divided but rather bring all the parts of who we are to every relationship and task before us.

Before we dive deeper, it's important to note that we're all prone to escapism and compartmentalization. We can see this tendency in the stay-at-home mom who loses her identity in meeting the needs of her husband and kids and feels good about herself only when her family feels good (also considered a form of codependency). Or in the thirty-six-year-old man who has been married for eight years, has three kids under six, is hugely successful at work, but is also having an emotional affair with his colleague because she is more fun, appreciates him, and makes him feel good about himself. We want to focus on how achievement outside the home can be one of the easiest pitfalls for men and women to escape to, especially when things at home don't come as easily, aren't as gratifying, or don't provide recognition.

THE ROLE OF WORK

To help unpack the toxic infection of escapism and the dangerous lie that leads to compartmentalized living, we need to examine key cultural factors likely influencing the rise of these realities. The first is the exponential increase in the number of men and women in the workplace. The second reality is that millennials (1980–2000)—at seventy-three million strong,[2] the largest adult generation in the US and the most recent to join the workforce—may often not be well equipped to navigate the stressors of life. One could make a case that the number of men and women vulnerable to escapism (as a way to achieve self-actualization and happiness) has never been greater.

As we focus on the millennial experience, note that we see millennials and their children as the future! We want to support and leverage all the strengths they bring to the table. Although some of the habits and addictions revealed in many millennials can be picked up by earlier generations (we know plenty of boomers and traditionalists addicted to their tablets and smartphones), contextual factors influence some generations more than others. It is critical that millennials effectively address the gaps inherited largely from their parents, who inherited their own gaps from their parents. We are proposing fresh insight to help secure a better future for all our kids.

GENERATIONAL INFLUENCES

These summaries are high-level descriptions of generational trends. The unique baggage millennials have inherited and grown up carrying makes them the most vulnerable to believing the lie and, in turn, escaping today. Their beliefs and behaviors will certainly create the baggage they hand off to their children. But don't think you're not influencing the next generations if you're a millennial and you choose not to marry or have kids. You may be their teacher, boss, youth leader, coach, or social media influencer. Remember, **if you have a following, you're a leader and how you live and lead matters.**

The trauma, triggers, and responses of one generation dramatically affect the beliefs and behaviors of subsequent generations. Beginning with the greatest generation (born 1910–27) and traditionalists (born 1928–45), a large population of men went to war while women and children stayed home. We admire so much about these generations: their courage, their commitment to duty, and their patriotism. But for so many, their adjustment back to civilian life was difficult. They became alcoholics to numb the pain and

PTSD from what they witnessed in battle. Their kids, the boomer generation (born 1946–64), were affected by their absence on the home front during the war and by a new layer of toxicity in the family system due to increased alcoholism used for coping (a form of escapism).

These children, the boomers, were shaped by the way things went down in their homes. Having lived through the effects of war on their parents and families, boomers protested the Vietnam War (sixties and early seventies) and escaped into the emerging landscapes of the workplace. Channeling the strong work ethic they inherited, they developed a more socially acceptable coping strategy through their careers. For the boomers, it wasn't war that ended marriages and tore families apart. No, their downfall was their ambition to climb the corporate ladder without processing their childhood wounds. This left the boomer generation with higher divorce rates than any previous generation.

The overworking of many boomers was due not so much to financial stress as to their generation's definition of success. Because boomers worked so much, they often bought their children stuff to make them "happy" instead of engaging with them relationally. Children were sent to daycare, where others played with them, educated them, and disciplined them (or didn't). Then, not having the energy to invest in their children or spend time camping, building things, or cooking together, burned-out boomer parents disengaged from their kids outside of work. (If you are a boomer, we're not trying to shame you here, as for some, working two or more jobs wasn't to pay for a Porsche. Remember, this is a thirty-thousand-foot view of generational markers, not every boomer's story.)

This brings us to the boomers' children, Gen X (1965–79). In general, they grew up in confusing homes, born into intact families that were later ripped apart by divorce. Gen Xers, in their own way, resisted the idea that work and climbing the ladder was the way to a better life. After witnessing corporate greed, cutthroat tactics, and inequity destroy relationships, primarily between them and their parents, Gen Xers used technology, innovation, and a lot of angst to escape and climb different ladders. They invented companies that could compete in the marketplace but also had values beyond the almighty buck. However, it would be the millennials, raised by those at the front end of the Gen X spectrum, who would be even more committed to connecting technology and innovation to causes.

Gen Xers were the first generation to comfortably engage with many emerging technologies, such as electronics, the internet, portable CD Discmans and later MP3 players, and an array of gaming systems. Easy access to technology funneled porn, abuse, and crime directly to our bedrooms. In this new reality, dark industries began to thrive like never before. It was easier to take what you wanted (think Napster) and stick it to those you thought did not deserve all the power, glory, and hype. Gen Xers would get it their way, and many tried relentlessly to stay ahead of getting caught.

TECH THROUGH THE GENERATIONS

When Gen Xers became parents, a new technology concern was introduced. Because of the absentee parenting modeled by their boomer parents, Gen Xers depended heavily on media such as *Sesame Street* and *Barney* to occupy their kids. But the momentary peace and quiet came at a huge cost. From an early age, millennials became used to depending too heavily on technology. Now, instead of disciplining kids and expecting them to behave in the grocery store, parents grab their phones or tablets, place them in their children's laps, and go back to shopping. Much as traditionalists assumed that smoking cigarettes was harmless, no one comprehended the extent of the new addictions and neurobiological changes in child development that would be created through using technology as a pacifier. Gen Xers and millennials would never say media raised their kids, but the truth is Americans in 2018 spent nearly half the hours they were awake in front of a screen of some sort.[3]

In this digital age, we are more connected than ever, yet we're lonelier because our basic human need for eye-to-eye compassionate connection isn't being met. Many millennials report that they felt lonely and unknown by their parents while growing up. They were left to figure out a lot of things on their own. Parents tried to provide private tutors, lessons, exclusive sports camps, prep schools, and the finest education money could buy, but those things were no substitute for parents who were present for their children in a healthy manner. Families who didn't have big wallets tried to keep up with everyone else. In fact, it could be argued that the advent of the Nintendo Entertainment System marked the day when parents and kids began to decline in intelligence, at least emotional intelligence. Fast-forward to what we know today about the harmful effects of gaming, digital devices, and addictive social media platforms, and we might realize that we have vast knowledge at our fingertips yet we lack critical thinking and relational IQ.

Mental health professionals and researchers are seeing many troubling correlations between social media and smartphone use and serious mental and behavioral disorders like severe anxiety, depression, bullying, and suicide. Every alert to a smartphone—whether a new text, email, or accepted friend request—triggers the brain to release dopamine. That may seem harmless, but research illuminates how people crave the feeling of pleasure caused by the release of dopamine and seek to increase the frequency. As the frequency increases, the brain gets used to it and requires more stimulus to satisfy the craving.[4] Young people have basically been handed "crack" the moment they could swipe a phone, and we are finally waking up to the consequences of our blind acceptance.

The law of diminishing returns helps us understand why we have a culture involved in escaping into sexting, pornography, online bullying, sex trafficking, violence on live feeds, and so much more—and at earlier ages. While craving dopamine, people are disconnected from their hearts, desensitized to consequences, and trying to find a sense of purpose—whether healthy or unhealthy, safe or unsafe, human or inhuman—through a device. All the increased exposure to firsthand tragedies results in higher levels of PTSD and lower empathy, both ways to compartmentalize the hurt.

THE FALLOUT

Millennials are the first generation to experience the digital age at their fingertips (internet, cell phones, interactive video gaming, smartphones) and all the world access that brings. Studies are showing that millennials may have more knowledge (or at least access to it), but they often lack wisdom attained from experiencing trials and tribulations, which develop character. These generational shifts have led to a culture where long-term character is no longer of interest, instead being replaced with values such as charisma, wit, and innovation. Smart devices provide instant windows into one another's lives, intensifying comparison and peer pressure. With so many family issues and outlets continually pumping unrealistic expectations into their minds, it's no wonder so many millennials struggle with ordinary aspects of life and cling to the unrealistic dream of fame to solve their dissatisfaction. Although credited with being the most educated generation in history, they are "considered to be generally narcissistic, immature and interested in short-term gratification."[5]

If you have not noticed the trend yet, trauma from one generation affects the next generation. This trauma will continue to harm families unless we do the personal work of shrinking our integrity gaps. Although life expectancy has increased, it wouldn't be hard to argue that quality of life has gotten worse! Sure, you may have a killer stock portfolio, three houses, kids at Ivy League schools, and a hot spouse. But ask yourself, Do you sleep well at night? Are you ignoring the signs of burnout? Are you addicted to your phone or things you access with it? We're finding more and more clients searching for peace of mind, a sense of satisfaction that money can't buy.

We are convinced that the overuse of technology is a contributing factor to the increase of diagnosable narcissistic personality disorder among millennials.[6] Mental health professionals and medical doctors alike have been concerned enough to make recommendations to the American Psychiatric Association to consider adding smartphone addiction and internet gaming addiction to the *Diagnostic and*

Statistical Manual of Mental Disorders. Former tech executives for Google, Facebook, YouTube, and other companies have blown the whistle on how these companies spend millions (maybe even billions) of dollars researching the human desire for the pleasure hormone dopamine in an effort to create applications, games, and interfaces that get people (primarily young people) hooked.[7] Now some of these tech leaders are investing their time and resources in solutions after seeing their own children fall victim to screen addiction, bullying, anxiety, depression, self-harm, and even suicide. They've become a voice for the development of nonaddictive hardware and software interfaces to prevent harm to coming generations.

We must learn to invest in face-to-face relationships with millennials and see the potential in these young men and women. When older generations enter, with permission, into their lives and connect knowledge with wisdom, millennials grow and gaps shrink for all parties. As we give them a vision for developing healthy attachment, trust, identity, and empathy, millennials heal and move toward healthy regulation and relationship building. Modeling how to turn off a screen at the end of the day in favor of a walk with a spouse or children brings peace—peace we all crave no matter what our generation.

Many readily acknowledge the need for mentorship among millennials. Celinne Da Costa, a millennial contributor to *Forbes*, said of her generation, "We need leaders who set us up for success, instill in us a sense of bigger purpose, and give us the confidence we need to persevere when the work gets challenging."[8] It's no wonder that "couples who participate in pre-marriage mentorship programs experience a 30 percent increase in marital success and fulfillment over those who don't participate."[9] Mentorship and character development are vital if we are going to see any shifts in the health of ourselves, our families, and our workplaces going forward. With each generation, we see an increased tendency to ignore our God-designed need for meaningful relationships at the center and put work, pleasure, or something else altogether at the forefront of our priorities.

> When older generations enter, with permission, into their lives and connect knowledge with wisdom, millennials grow and gaps shrink for all parties.

Whether the struggle is recovering from literal war or wars online, our inclination to escape outside the home and give our best to those beyond our own living rooms is creating a long-term leadership crisis we need to address head-on. In her well-known and groundbreaking TED talk on vulnerability in 2010, Brené Brown reminded us that we are more addicted and numbed out than ever before in western history.[10] We as humans—and leaders in particular—are prone to compartmentalizing our personal and professional lives and seeking to meet our root-level needs outside the home. Our priorities have turned on their heads, and we idealize being happy, living out our dreams, and being all we can be more than faithfulness, commitment, perseverance, tenacity, and good old-fashioned grit.

IN THE BIBLE

Each generation since the garden of Eden has had a bent toward wanting more than what's before them. However, this deep-seated disappointment spurs us to try to meet our own needs without God or others. Noah, honored in the Bible's Hall of Faith (see Heb. 11:7), was a righteous man who trusted and obeyed God. For 120 years, he worked diligently on the ark as his community ridiculed him. During the flood that God had promised, Noah and his family lived for more than a year on the ark before they could return to land. The trauma he and his family must have experienced was enormous. In his shortsightedness and deep pain over all he had been through, Noah's humanity finally caught up with him, and his son found him drunk in a tent (see Gen. 9:21–22). For some, this might be too far of a leap, but we try to empathize with all that Noah had carried. Although his work had great purpose and meaning—literal life-and-death significance—the weight of giving one's life to work combined with survivor's guilt might drive anyone to drink too much.

The temptation to compartmentalize—to emotionally and physically separate from the reality of our situations—lies in all of us. Leaders can have a high capacity to keep going toward a goal regardless of the cost. But even Noah, a man of great character who was marked by his faithfulness to God regardless of ridicule, struggled to cope in the end. Beyond numbing out from our work or succumbing to temptations related to drinking, technology, sex, food, or whatever, self-preservation seeps into even the greatest of leaders when push comes to shove. Our families are the ones who pay for our lack of processing and self-care.

Abraham, another righteous Hall of Faith man (see Heb. 11:8–12), was chosen by God to be the father of many nations. Make yourself familiar with his story in Genesis 12–25. God told Abraham He would make him a great nation and commanded, "Go from your country, your people and your father's household to the land I will show you" (12:1). Like any good leader, he followed God. The lineage of Jesus is traced back to Abraham, and God did keep His word to Abraham. However, Abraham lied, not once but twice, telling rulers that his wife was his sister so they would not kill him. Abraham put his wife in extreme danger, giving her to other men. Not only was that an incredible form of compartmentalization, it was also abusive. Though culturally normal, Abraham sought his own wisdom to cover his needs and justify his behaviors.[11] I think we can learn from Abraham's self-preservation and failure to go to God and trust His ways and timing.

> Compartmentalizing is just another clever way to protect our hearts from being disappointed, feeling devalued, or experiencing insignificance.

We bring up these two faith heroes, who were both great leaders with a desire to please and honor God, to demonstrate how easy it is for any of us to run from pain. No matter how humble or great the call on our lives, our humanity is right before us. We must acknowledge our needs as well as humble ourselves to see how our behaviors, goals, and even purpose affect the lives of those we say we love the most. Our offices have been filled with inspiring leaders who the world sees as *a-mazing* yet whose own families find it hard to appreciate them when at the end of the day all they get is crumbs. Compartmentalizing is just another clever way to protect our hearts from being disappointed, feeling devalued, or experiencing insignificance. Though common, it is not healthy.

(Terra) I have dedicated my life to helping people move through trauma, which requires being a witness and joining in the grieving. As a leader of a company, therapist, author, speaker, and social entrepreneur, I was reaching my own personal Noah breakdown with secondary PTSD from all the wreckage I was seeing. Toward my fifteenth year in private practice, by the time I would get home—working with clients only two days a week—I was done. If my daughters had minor concerns, I had little to no empathy left for them. Jeff became the one who was there for me, and I forgot he had needs too. My egocentric humanity was in preservation mode, showing up as irritable, impatient, and always wanting to sleep.

One day Jeff said that I was no longer myself and he missed me. My tender heart that had once led me to dive into deep waters with hurting folks had turned hard. **It was a wake-up call that I needed to do some of my own work, as I had compartmentalized my worth, focusing only on the good I was doing with those outside my home. This was a "shrinking the integrity gap" moment for me.** God promptly reminded me of a time in my early twenties when I was with other aspiring leaders, listening to humble stories of moral failures and missteps from more experienced leaders. I remembered that, in declaring my call to help leaders live with integrity and help their families survive the beast of leadership, I would not forsake my own. I did not want to be everyone else's hero and find my own family rolling their eyes on the sidelines.

THE CALL

Being an "old soul," I relate to the older generation in so many ways even though I have been raised in a culture that appreciates efficiency and making money for a cause. And like many millennials, Jeff and I have given our lives to social entrepreneurship, limiting our profits for the greater good of our community. In the work we have done and are seeking to do, we are committed to keeping the good of others in mind. We have also wanted to live out of our priorities and not give in to the workaholism that would easily overtake us both if we were left to our own bents.

Cultivating rich and meaningful relationships in our home far outweighs the impact we can have on the next generation through our work. Mother Teresa, seen by every generation as one of the most influential leaders, once said, "It is easy to love the people far away. It is not always easy to love those close to us.... Bring love into your home for this is where our love for each other must start."[12] Our homes and closest friendships are where we can nourish intimate relationship with God and others in the most tangible ways, and these relationships will launch us to have our greatest impact on the generations to come.

Escaping from our most intimate relationships and compartmentalizing pain through performance is as old as the garden of Eden. In Noah and Abraham, who both returned to God and others after they royally messed up, and from Genesis through Revelation we see that repairing relationships is possible. If we are going to see a decline in escapism and the harmful effects of living compartmentalized lives, then older generations must reach back to younger generations and connect those generations' vast knowledge with their own real-time wisdom. We need to be pressing into real relationships where we laugh, play, cry, talk, listen, and feel ordinary moments together.

     We all need to stop pretending everything is perfect and instead talk about real leaders, couples, friends, and families who faced adversity and became closer through it. We all benefit from seeing people who identified shortcomings in their lives, did their deeper work, and are now reaping the rewards of growth, health, and maturity. Let's talk more about what it looks like to recognize the error of our ways earlier and commit to being on the solution side! It's going to take a lot of mentors to invest in seventy-three million millennials and the rising generation of their children. We can all just blame other generations, cultural shifts, or our fathers and mothers. Or we can lean into our pain, find help, and learn to be the kind of leaders we are desperate to see … and would want to live with at the end of the day.

Key Markers of Escapism and Compartmentalization

• You ignore a nagging spouse, struggling children, and even disdain from older teens and adult children.
• You continually work long hours and make excuses for why you are needed elsewhere.

• You need to be "doing something" and have a difficult time with quiet or solitude.

• You cope with overeating, excessive use of media, harmful leisure activities (including pornography), substance abuse, etc.

• You are always too busy and respond to the asks of those in your inner circle with "Tomorrow," "Next week," or "Not now."

• You want (or prefer) the attention those outside your home are giving you.

Antidotes

1. Shrinking our integrity gaps means we resist this subtle lie: *I need to protect my heart from pain, and I can control the variables relating to all the hats I wear in a way that produces maximum happiness for me.* How have you bought into this lie, and how are you resisting its temptations?

2. On a sheet of paper or in a journal, create concentric circles (see appendix B for a sample). Think about who and what in your life is most important to you, and list them from your top priority at the center out to each larger circle. In each circle, write how you spend your time intentionally investing in these areas. The most central circle should be God and your relationship with Him. (Is it? Be honest.) The next for many might be marriage (or a future spouse). Then if you have kids, your children likely come next. Maybe your extended family or work follows. Then list your friends, church, and community. When we see our values in order, we can quickly see

whether we are living out of balance and trying to meet outer circle needs before we consider those in the inner circles.

3. List your primary personal needs. Then write out how you are meeting each of those needs. Put a star near the ones that seem healthy and an exclamation mark near those that are detracting from your health (emotionally, mentally, physically, or relationally). If you think you do not have needs, then maybe ask a mentor or counselor to help you identify them.

4. Write out what you love about your work. Name what you dislike about your work. This will help you assess where you may be working against your God-given design in order to climb the ladder.

5. Find a millennial (or a younger person, if you are a millennial who has done your work) to start meeting with regularly. Invest your life into theirs. Be there for him or her. If this person is your son or daughter, it's even more important to share who you are and how you handled similar things growing up rather than giving a mini lecture on what he or she should do. Young people are desperate to learn and grow (even if they pretend to know it all). Share your lows and highs, and listen to understand his or her lows and highs. Resist the urge to teach lessons. Mentoring in relationship is about what the other person needs and wants.

Chapter 6

NARCISSISM

I Think I'm Pretty Amazing

*Do nothing out of selfish ambition or vain conceit. Rather,
in humility value others above yourselves, not looking to your
own interests but each of you to the interests of the others.*
—Philippians 2:3–4

Narcissism is a word that gets tossed around a fair amount. In our experience, most leaders have some narcissistic tendencies. Actually, most humans do … it's called a sin nature. "I want my way." We do not know a human being who comes out of the womb and says, "Sure, Mom, you sleep before my needs get met. You have been working hard to care for me; it's your time to rest." The natural bent of all humanity is "me first." When narcissists interact with others, they automatically make those interactions about themselves. Like holding up a mirror, a narcissist can see only his or her own reflection in every interaction. Over time, when nurtured well, many people learn how to see beyond themselves and develop empathy for others. However, a narcissist never develops empathy and uses people as a means to an end. Allowing this bent to go unchecked harms those in this leader's wake, who are left feeling abused, used, disoriented, and hollowed out with little understanding of why.

There is a distinct difference between being "me" centered and having true narcissistic personality disorder (NPD). According to DSM-5, NPD is characterized by "a pervasive pattern of grandiosity (in fantasy or behavior), need for admiration, and lack of empathy."[1] Narcissism is not something we are born with but rather something we can develop as young as two years old, when extreme trauma, a lack of boundaries, entitlement, and emotional neglect create a complex response in us. Narcissists grow up in all kinds of homes but particularly in performance-based families that value image over intimate relationships. Their self-esteem becomes inflated, empathy is not modeled, and they have little to no ability to see beyond their own circumstances. All children lack the internal skills to navigate the needs of others and must be taught throughout childhood.

Those who study narcissism have learned that it manifests along a continuum rather than as a definitive yes-or-no diagnosis. The degree of its manifestation can make or break whether a narcissist is able to maintain any healthy connections. What is even more fascinating is that of all people with personality disorders, people with NPD are typically the most adored, liked, and full of charisma.[2] Narcissists learn to dazzle with their charm, skills, and power until someone decides to dislike them or—God forbid—disagree with them. Because of the cultural shift from character to charisma, permissive parenting, participation trophies, and social media empires built on selfies, the narcissistic personality spectrum is more common today. The effects are widespread, creating power differentials in every relationship. From marriage to parenting to organizational teams, those in relationship with a narcissist are often emotionally, psychologically, and spiritually abused. The toxicity is often disguised for years, and those in his or her wake have some ambivalence about the relationship.

STORIES OF NARCISSISM

(Terra) Narcissists rarely end up in the counseling office on their own. Typically, spouses or children bring them in after first undertaking a tremendous amount of preparation and healing on their part. People with true NPD will stay in counseling only to get the results they want in their marriages and families and will make every effort to avoid changing their egocentric way of life by using tactics such as anger, intimidation, and shame.

One of the first narcissists I worked with was a well-loved Christian leader in the area. His deeply shamed family needed a confidential space to unpack why they could not think, feel, or act without his approval. No one would suspect that his family was suffering, as they had all learned to play the part of a model family and did not know another way. Telling anyone outside of counseling not only felt like severe betrayal of their husband and dad but also felt like betrayal of themselves. This family was in therapy for three years before the narcissist was willing to come into session. This leader was going to lose everything unless he faced the root of his power-and-control matrix. When he began sharing, his story was one of the worst I had ever heard. He had learned from the young age of two that no one, not even God, should be trusted. Learning to empathize with and have compassion for his family started only when he could grieve the travesty of the little boy who had experienced severe abuse and neglect. His powerful gifts of teaching and wooing others were dysfunctional ways of protecting himself from submitting to and being influenced or harmed by anyone—not God, not his wife, and surely not any other leader or friend.

I recently interviewed an incredible woman of God and influencer named Shauna. She humbly shared an experience similar to that of many other men and women I have walked alongside. She spent years thinking it was her fault that her husband, a pastor at several well-known churches, was having affairs. His anger and clever ways of narrating a story kept her confused, insecure, and working hard to be the wife he claimed to always want. Now divorced many years, Shauna said that she did not blame her younger self for trying so hard to save their marriage but, looking back, she recognized that her ex-husband was a covert narcissist and a master manipulator. When she tried to tell leaders in their church, they quickly responded to keep the blowup under control but did little to help her and her kids or to address his destructive behaviors. He was eventually let go and immediately moved into other roles of power and influence where he could recreate his image and continue to try to control the outcomes.

Research is showing that the number of leaders with undiagnosed NPD is much higher than realized. In their sobering book *Let Us Prey: The Plague of Narcissist Pastors and What We Can Do about It*, Glenn Ball and Darrell Puls reported that out of 1,380 active and retired clergy surveyed in just one Canadian denomination, almost 30 percent met the diagnostic criteria for NPD![3] Imagine if this trend translated to every denominational presence in Canada and the

United States. You may have worked for one or more of these leaders and not known it until now. A narcissist may have been the founder of a business you worked for or the original pastor of a church you attended. The narcissists you've encountered likely had charisma that drew people to them. No one, except those in their inner circles or those who got in their way, would ever guess that they had such a large integrity gap. Narcissistic leaders work hard to protect their image and their narrative of reality.

✦ **Key markers of a narcissist are a perpetual lack of empathy, little remorse, entitlement, deception, control, and required admiration and emotional support.** They use tactics like gaslighting, minimizing, flattering, and controlling to get their needs met at all costs. Gaslighting is "a form of psychological abuse used by narcissists in order to instill in their victims an extreme sense of anxiety and confusion to the point where they no longer trust their own memory, perception or judgment."[4]

(Jeff) These traits may explain why it can be so hard (or impossible) for persons with NPD to actually hear any level of criticism about themselves. I was present during an intervention when a male with NPD was confronted with a list of physical and sexual abuses he had committed against the survivor. He had no response. It was as if he could not hear the charges being made against him so they didn't exist. The first words out of his mouth (and for the next two hours as he dissociated) were about something entirely unrelated to what had just been shared, despite the fact that the accusations had been written in a letter for him to reference and the confrontation was being witnessed by several others in the room. He was running from reality, something he had been doing for more than five decades.

DETECTING NARCISSISTS

Although narcissistic leaders are likely more prevalent in our businesses, schools, and places of worship than we think, it is not easy to detect them. How can we be more aware of narcissistic leaders in our midst? One answer may be to spend more time studying actual servant-leaders as a contrast. The US Treasury Department uses a similar approach to track down counterfeiters. They give a special group the responsibility of confidently recognizing a counterfeit bill when they see one. To train their eyes and other senses to detect a fraud, it's essential for them to spend more time studying the real thing than the fake.[5]

As hard as it can be to identify narcissistic leaders, they exhibit some recurring behaviors. At home, a narcissist uses his spouse to meet all his emotional and physical needs, taking all the oxygen for himself. His needs are all consuming (including sex), and when confronted (which is rare in this dynamic), he will defend himself, criticize others, and twist the narrative so his spouse is always the problem. The spouses of narcissists often say they feel crazy, as they have lost sight of their own needs, wants, and hopes. In Christian circles a narcissist's spouse often looks like a loyal and dutiful supporter who quietly serves in the background.

At work, a leader might exert her authority more overtly to preserve the image that the success of the business is largely (if not entirely) due to her. Narcissists constantly assign praise and success to themselves but never any blame; mistakes are always due to someone else's incompetence. Because it's not socially acceptable to be a narcissist, they try to steer others' perceptions of them as far from the idea as possible. To those on the outside, the narcissistic leader tries to control the narrative: her business is the best place to work; her company is winning in the marketplace; its success can largely be linked to her. However, when something goes wrong, the narcissistic leader will quickly find a scapegoat to avoid any personal responsibility. Narcissists intentionally use deception to remain in power and have no remorse about how they achieve the results they desire. The cost is enormous. Sir Walter Scott may have said it best: "O what a tangled web we weave, / When first we practise to deceive!"[6]

Similarly in the church, the narcissistic leader is committed to image maintenance: filled seats, strong donors (who ironically can also be narcissists concerned with their image and influence), and little to no mess. As places where rules without relationship and charisma without accountability tend to reign, churches provide safe spaces for narcissists at any point on the spectrum to thrive. Leaders often use God's name and His grace to continue using and abusing. It doesn't help that due diligence is lacking in our hiring processes in the church. Narcissistic Christian leaders can easily hide and create environments where they perpetrate some of the worst abuses. They have an insatiable appetite for self-soothing because of their small egos (similar to those of two-year-olds). So the praise, adoration, and worship found in ministry environments provide the appetizer, main course, and dessert to continuously feed that unhealthy hunger to get their needs met. The sickening part is that their behavior regularly ends up being accepted and fostered for years while others are abused.

Shame from the covert abuse in narcissistic systems can cause survivors to have chronic low self-worth and leave them vulnerable to other abusive dynamics. "Shame resulting from childhood abuse

has ... been shown to be strongly associated with adult revictimiza-
tion and adult depression."[7] The spouses and children of narcissists
are often revictimized in other systems (work, church, marriage, etc.)
if they do not get help to restore their sense of identity. Accustomed
to having no voice, no value, and no power, survivors believe they
need the narcissist in order to know who they are and what to do
next. This belief creates an unhealthy attachment, constant low-grade
depression, an acute sense of hopelessness, and a deep-seated feeling
of despair that life will always be this way. Survivors suffer a deep loss
of identity and dignity and often blame themselves for these feelings,
protecting the narcissist at all costs.

Ironically, narcissists also struggle with deep-seated shame, but
it creates an opposite response in them. Instead of seeing themselves
as powerless and worthless, they believe they are the most important
one in the room and deserve more. They tend to focus only on how
everyone is performing, often trying hard to keep others from looking beneath the surface. Any sense of genuine intimacy is sabotaged
by a lack of awareness of self and others and an enormous fear of
losing all their power.

Whether the narcissist or the victim, healing is possible by submitting to what God says about them. Tracy explained, "The key
to overcoming shame [the root of all abuse] is more than simply
learning to love and accept oneself; it is to discern God's perspective
on one's shame and guilt, and to let his perspective drive and reshape
one's thoughts, actions, and, ultimately, one's feelings."[8] The struggle
here is that the narcissist does not want to hear the opinion of God—
or of anyone else for that matter. The Word says the truth will set us
free (see John 8:32). "Truth" is *alētheia* in Greek, often translated as

"unconcealedness" or "disclosure."[9] The hardest thing for a narcissist to live with is truth (about themselves, others, and God), an aversion that creates a thick barrier to healing and health.

ABUSE IN THE CHURCH

Christ is the head of the church and is worshipped because of His sovereignty, power, righteousness, and sacrificial love, among many other attributes. But who is next in line in most churches in America? The pastor is present in the flesh, leading the church in the practices of worship, service, discipleship, evangelism, and prayer. Because of the human tendency to fall into the trap of hero worship, predatory narcissists find a refuge and lifeline inside local churches and Christian organizations, where they seek to get their own needs met rather than care for their flocks. "Christians must take the implications of universal depravity seriously and accept the fact that *all* humans are capable of abuse."[10]

Narcissistic leaders are often the abusers in the church, using their charisma as a grooming tactic and their intelligence and confidence to get their victims in a place of powerlessness. These primary offenders perpetuate emotional neglect, psychological mind games, and oppressive power. Entire communities will hide abusers' harmful behaviors, which empowers the abusers at the expense of others. Whether from overt abuse (sexual and physical) or covert abuse and neglect (spiritual, emotional, and psychological), victims are left with haunting scars that can cover them with despair and shame.

Kimi Harris wrote an article in *Christianity Today* exposing how sex offenders, many of whom are narcissistic, groom the church because of the church's lack of education about abuse and mental health. Grooming is "strategically manipulat[ing] the victim, their family, and the community to hide ... deviant intentions and avoid detection."[11] A study found that "the community itself can also be primed and controlled through the grooming process. Many offenders tend to adopt a pattern of socially responsible and caring behavior in public. They endeavour to build a good reputation and to create a strong social perception of themselves as being an upstanding member of the local church or community, as a nice man."[12] In an interview for the article, Terra "explained how abusers will exploit Christian principles of forgiveness and grace for their own end and use any spiritual authority to override people feeling uncomfortable or resisting their grooming. If they are caught in one church, they simply move on." She went on to say, "Many offenders start over and over, finding communities that forgive quickly, offer grace to any kind of story, and do little in terms of investigating a person's history. Often these churches will only resource themselves with the Bible and remain uneducated about trauma and abuse because 'God will take care of it.' This is not only irresponsible, but church leaders that do this are exposing their communities to the potential for real harm."[13]

"Abusers cannot be predicted by race, occupation, demeanor, education level, or facial features."[14] Since so many narcissistic leaders are put into positions of leadership because of their capacity and skill, along with their exceptional charisma, the danger lies in not being educated and trauma informed. The church's comprehension of trauma is important for so many reasons. Tracy said being trauma informed helps us understand how people heal after they have been abused, why abuse has such long-term effects, why victims often are so dead emotionally, spiritually, and relationally, and why we should not blame abuse victims for their trauma responses. "Researchers have gradually come to understand that all forms of trauma, be it domestic violence, sexual abuse, war, or natural disasters, create extreme stress, which can result in a variety of debilitating emotional and physical symptoms."[15]

> Because of the human tendency to fall into the trap of hero worship, predatory narcissists find a refuge and lifeline inside local churches and Christian organizations, where they seek to get their own needs met rather than care for their flocks.

Experts who work with offenders have created a universally known profile to help identify potential abusers. Abusers usually possess a pervasive ability to deny responsibility, regardless of how small or large the accusations. One of the most chilling examples of a narcissistic abusive leader is Adolf Eichmann, a Nazi official. "Over and over Adolph Eichmann declared he was not criminally responsible for the murder of millions of Jews in Nazi death camps, for he was simply 'following orders.'"[16] Tracy says, "Rapists sometimes blame victims for dressing seductively. Date rapists invariably say the sex was consensual, physical abusers blame family members for making them mad." He goes on to report two studies detailing the fact that sexual abusers will deny responsibility because of their own pain (excuses like "I am being deprived in my own marriage") or blame their victims (children or adults), saying they consented, instigated the behavior, or initiated contact. Studies show abusers using statements like "I never beat my wife. I responded physically to her."[17]

Why are we talking so much about abuse survivors when the topic is narcissistic leaders? (1) Most narcissists are severe-abuse survivors. (2) Abuse survivors are the most vulnerable to narcissistic leaders. Trauma skews our ability to trust, often causing us to trust what is untrustworthy and mistrust what is trustworthy. Narcissistic systems are generally marked by a leader (dad, husband, wife, mother, pastor, CEO) who has all the answers and has attracted a following who need that leader in order to find self-worth, security, and meaning in life. The healthier a survivor gets, the more he or she realizes the narcissist is not safe or healthy. The survivor ends up either creating havoc in a system or leaving and being left with haunting triggers.

Whether churches with "star" pastors or businesses with CEOs who always know the right direction, organizational systems that squash doubt, questioning, processing, variation, or dialogue are vulnerable to the narcissistic leader. One of the most common warning signs is leaders who consistently guilt others for creativity or questioning their decisions or behavior. They assert that those who are mature and faithful will align themselves with the needs of the church and their vision. But narcissists are about only themselves and leave their sheep in poor condition.

PROTECTING THE CHURCH

Though leaders who are wolves in sheep's clothing may come and plunder the sheep, God is watching over His people and will provide a way out. Sometimes the way out is clearly calling out a wolf. Listen to Ezekiel 34:2–10:

> Woe to you shepherds of Israel who only take care of yourselves! Should not shepherds take care of the flock? You eat the curds, clothe yourselves with the wool and slaughter the choice animals, but you do not take care of the flock. You have not strengthened the weak or healed the sick or bound up the injured. You have not brought back the strays or searched for the lost. You have ruled them harshly and brutally. So they were scattered because there was no shepherd, and when they were scattered they became food for all the wild animals. My sheep wandered over all the mountains and on every high hill. They were scattered over the whole earth, and no one searched or looked for them.
>
> Therefore, you shepherds, hear the word of the LORD: As surely as I live, declares the Sovereign LORD, because my flock lacks a shepherd and so has been plundered and has become food for all the wild animals, and because my shepherds did not search for my flock but cared for themselves rather than for my flock, therefore, you shepherds, hear

the word of the LORD: This is what the Sovereign
LORD says: I am against the shepherds and will hold
them accountable for my flock. I will remove them
from tending the flock so that the shepherds can
no longer feed themselves. I will rescue my flock
from their mouths, and it will no longer be food
for them.

The good news is that in verses 29–31 God said,

I will provide for them a land renowned for its
crops, and they will no longer be victims of famine
in the land or bear the scorn of the nations. Then
they will know that I, the LORD their God, am with
them and that they, the Israelites, are my people,
declares the Sovereign LORD. You are my sheep, the
sheep of my pasture, and I am your God, declares
the Sovereign LORD.

**Wise is the church that builds in accountability checks and
balances to help deter and defend against abusive tendencies
and those who would abuse within the ministry environment.**
It is key for elder boards to have term limits as well as processes and
covenants that align with scriptural principles. It would also be wise
for male-dominated elder boards to regularly consult with women
leaders. If you maintain the view that only men can fill the biblical
role of elder, you also must remember that all of us were created in
God's image, both male and female. Anyone in leadership in the

church or elsewhere would be wise to consider the opposite sex when drafting ideas, making decisions, communicating, disciplining, or engaging in any other leadership behavior affecting both genders. We will be held to account as leaders for how we stewarded the roles and responsibilities God gave us and how we treated others, who were created in His image, especially in His name.

AM I A NARCISSIST?

If you're asking yourself whether you're a narcissistic leader, good! That is a great place to start examining where you are. Truth is, most narcissists won't even ask that question because they cannot bear to see a less-than-perfect image of themselves. Narcissists are unlikely to truly repent of narcissism unless they are on the low end of the continuum. It is our hope and prayer that you are asking yourself this question early in your journey—ideally in your undergraduate years or earlier! Remember, most leaders in any organization (secular or sacred) have some characteristics that look like narcissism. For example, dreamers can look grandiose. Confidence can look like arrogance. Paul the apostle could be seen as a narcissistic Pharisee whose heart was transformed and whose self-focused righteousness was redeemed in an assurance of faith and unwavering determination. Here are the key questions to consider:

1. Do I willingly allow others to lead me?
2. Do I allow outside ideas and contributions to have an impact on my life?
3. Do I own my failures without excuses or reasons?

If you sincerely engage in these suggested initiatives (more in the antidotes), good for you. Instead of praying about everyone else's responses, ask God and others for regular feedback. (Remember King Saul?) Honestly share with two or three friends regarding the negative characteristics you feel conviction about, and allow those friends to help you grow in addition to affirming you. Narcissists will come dressed in false humility to get their needs met in an unhealthy way (tending to the sheep for their own pleasure or to make it look like they care), and their friends won't even know they are adding to the problem! When was the last time a friend asked you for feedback on anything he or she might need to work on? In general, it's a rare practice and that's sad.

Narcissists love a good book or follow popular leaders (successful ones, of course). Instead of actually seeking to mature and develop for the purpose of serving others, they absorb knowledge to mimic others who are successful! Consider why you read and learn from others. Remember, narcissists have small egos and are unsure of who they are. They will mirror or model other leaders. Having the right books (including the Bible) means nothing if a person doesn't apply the wisdom contained in those books for the right reasons.

Finally, a narcissist will likely consider mentorship only if it meets a need for himself or herself. Consider your motive for mentorship and whether you are willing to receive feedback. It's rare for narcissists to submit to authentic mentorship for an extended period of time. In the context of a positive and safe relationship, serious mentors will address areas in the lives of mentees that need improvement. If narcissists feel they've gotten the knowledge or experience they wanted from the mentor relationship, they're likely done and will claim the wisdom as their own. After all, they got what they came for (at least they think so!).

This relates to the discussion in the previous chapter—many emerging leaders need mentorship because of the environmental and parenting circumstances that have led to so many narcissistic tendencies. Many didn't get their relational needs met at home, so they sought to get them met in other ways (Facebook, Snapchat, Twitter, etc.) that create addiction and isolation rather than real face-to-face relationships. Though we hesitate to leap to any conclusions, this narcissistic/abuse cycle might correlate to the younger generations and the starstruck phenomenon. Hungry for structure and mentorship, they are more vulnerable to charisma over character.

SHRINKING THIS GAP

If we want fewer leaders with narcissistic tendencies in the workplace, government, places of worship, and our communities, we must invest in real relationships with younger generations. We must cultivate empathy and embrace a holistic type of leadership where character matters and consequences are experienced. Teaching the difference between performing and personhood, establishing the importance of give-and-take relationships, and practicing convicted civility are all ways we can unite to guard against power-hungry, narcissistic leaders.

It would be awesome to see God supernaturally zap an entire generation with maturity, selflessness, and healthy coping strategies. However, what is more realistic, as Henry Cloud and John Townsend suggested in their book *How People Grow*, is that "relationship is the primary place people can grow."[18] As they say, that's God's plan A;

instantly effecting change in people's lives is not.[19] The tricky part of needing other people in our lives to help us grow is the matter of trust. In fact, our friends at Trueface Ministries would say maturity happens in relationships of trust and environments of grace.[20] How many people do you actually trust to help you grow? As John Gottman stated, "Trust is … an essential part of social influence—the idea being that it is easier to influence those who trust us."[21] And in order to help others grow, we must be safe and trustworthy recipients of their requests for help and counsel.

> We must cultivate empathy and embrace a holistic type of leadership where character matters and consequences are experienced.

In order for narcissists on the lower end of the continuum to move from self-protecting and controlling to receiving care, love, and eventually trust, someone in their system must find help first. Their spouse. Their children. Their staff. It's usually someone being oppressed by the narcissist. Depending on the value of the relationship, narcissists may engage in a process of healing if they get to start on their own terms. Clear and well-defined boundaries are necessary. Many clients and their families have been in the healing process anywhere from four to seven years. It can take an enormous amount of time to unravel the confusing messages and rebuild the walls that multiple generations have demolished. When we understand that a narcissist is a trauma survivor who either is reasserting power in order to avoid ever being hurt again or is using people as a means to get personal needs met, then healing relies on a slow and steady reparenting approach.

THE CALL

Whether you're a leader who recognizes your own narcissistic tendencies and is working on keeping them in check or you feel you likely have a deeper challenge with narcissism (or have been diagnosed with NPD), there is hope! Do what you can to take healthy, wise, and practical steps to shrink your integrity gap. For some, the steps we recommend here will do wonderful things in your life and in the lives of those you care about. Others of you need to schedule that first counseling appointment and share with a trusted friend that you are stepping toward getting practical help. Ask that friend to hold you accountable for staying in the work that will likely get harder before it ever gets easier. If you meet the criteria for diagnosable NPD, then you need to learn how to:

1. stay in reality
2. understand the triggers that lead you to self-protect
3. develop and maintain healthy relationships
4. create a regular support system to protect you in times of vulnerability

When someone awakens to the reality that he or she has been using people as a means of self-protecting because of past wounds, a miracle has happened—and God still does miracles!

Healing takes time, consistency of community, submission to the process and to others, and a humility that will feel like fighting every step of the way. The "two-year-old" will of a narcissist has to relearn how to trust, and it does not look pretty in a full-fledged adult. This is your best chance of experiencing greater health and wholeness in your journey. It's also the best chance others in your life have of experiencing that health and wholeness with you! If you're a younger leader who has discovered that you are serving under a narcissist, seek counsel ASAP. This confusing relationship is too hard to untangle alone. Action may include setting up boundaries or shifting environments, and depending on the length of the relationship, grief and trauma healing may be needed.

We are praying for you as we are also protecting you and your sheep in Jesus' name. The assurance and peace we hold on to is that for those who confess and repent (turn away with actions and results) from their selfish and habitually sinful ways, God is faithful and more than just in His grace to remove the eternal consequences of our sin (see 1 John 1:9). For those who do not confess or repent (the crux for a narcissist), He is perfectly just and able to hold them accountable for their action or inaction. The opportunity to receive grace, forgiveness, and life-changing help from Jesus is available to us right now. Knowing this: what we do in this lifetime impacts eternity. Consider your need for Jesus' help. He is your only hope. That's the truth for all of us!

Key Markers of Narcissism

- You perpetually lack empathy (see only your own perspective).
- You feel little remorse when confronted.

Narcissism 135

- You have high expectations and feel entitled.
- You are great at deception and presenting in order to meet your own agenda.
- You crave admiration and emotional support and are highly controlling. (You are either for me or against me.)
- You use tactics like gaslighting, minimizing, flattery, and power plays to get your needs met and self-protect at all costs.

Antidotes

About the narcissist:

1. A narcissist will often not confess, so he or she may need to be confronted by a group. Narcissists are clever about appeasing the audiences they speak with, so having everyone in the room is often important.

2. If the narcissist is willing to seek counsel, recognize that this person will need a slow and steady approach to therapy. Often the best clinical fit is a trauma-informed therapist who has experience working with narcissists. Some narcissists have developed their skills so well that they enjoy the risk and challenge of matching wits with experts. Keeping them in therapy is the hardest part, so recognize that it may take years to see change.

To the survivor of a narcissist:

1. Educate yourself on narcissism. Now that you understand there is a continuum, recognize the key differences between a broken and

contrite heart like David's and the heart of someone like Saul—sad because of getting caught.

2. How a person responds to being confronted is a key sign of whether change and healing in the relationship are possible. If the person responds with anger, blame, or shame, do not confront him or her alone.

3. Write a list describing who you are apart from the narcissist in your life. Often individuals married to, parented by, or in mentoring relationships with narcissists have the hardest time recognizing their own identity. This step may require time and some intentional grieving first.

4. Set healthy boundaries. If you have been a victim of someone with true NPD, staying in relationship with that person is not possible until you can have emotional, physical, and spiritual autonomy.

5. Recognizing narcissistic systems as abuse can help you identify the healing journey you might need to take before you are able to trust God, yourself, and others again.

To help reduce any narcissistic tendencies, you might consider the following:[22]

- Ask God to reveal to you any narcissistic tendencies, and ask for His help to address them.

- Share these tendencies with one to three friends or mentors, and ask them what they see in you.
- Ask these trusted sources for practical ideas to help you address these narcissistic tendencies.
- Read more Christian leadership books, listen to speakers, and follow leaders on social media who are addressing integrity and character development. (Remember not to put an unhealthy amount of faith or hope in *one* person other than Jesus Christ.)
- Ask God to provide you with a mentor who exhibits humility, integrity, and servant leadership in his or her sphere of influence, whether in business or ministry. Ask this person to prayerfully consider mentoring you. This mentor needs to be able to tell you the truth. (Remember once again not to put an unhealthy amount of faith or hope in *one* person.)

Chapter 7

ARROGANCE

I'm Better Than Everyone Else

All have their worth ... and each contributes to the worth of the others.
—J. R. R. Tolkien, *The Silmarillion*

Swallow your pride. / You will not die; it's not poison.
—Bob Dylan, "Tombstone Blues"

Healthy leaders build healthy teams. Healthy teams value everyone on the team and each person's unique contributions. No one appreciates superstars who believe they make or break their teams (even if they do). In truth, arrogance reminds us of narcissism, but it's a more common temptation for leaders. *Arrogance* is defined as "an attitude of superiority manifested in an overbearing manner or in presumptuous claims or assumptions."[1] It naturally feels good to have people look to us for direction and wisdom, but when our vision starts to grow, pride is right there knocking on the door. Scripture warns against arrogance, and depending on a person's story and how that person is hardwired, temptation presents itself in a variety of ways: *I am smarter, faster, wiser, better, etc.* Arrogant leaders think they know what is best the majority of the time and rarely seek wise counsel, to the point of sincerely believing they are more intelligent than the rest of their teams and those in their wake. Regardless, self-importance sabotages the greater good of the community. In contrast, Wholehearted Leaders stay humble and recognize that accomplishments result from God's power and the contributions of others along the way.

(Jeff) A few years ago, I was brought in to work with a team of professionals who had started a business in an exciting and emerging industry in Oregon. Their CEO had been identified by a number of magazines and other media sources as the new face of the industry. A lot of buzz surrounded this young prodigy and his company, but with less than twenty full-time employees trying to manage the intense growth, everyone was pretty fried.

The first time I walked through the front door, I toured the facility with the CEO, Chris, who was in his early thirties. He was a confident leader, with some hint of arrogance, and enjoyed exposing the colorful eye-candy of the decor as we passed through doors and hallways. Expansions, build-outs, and construction areas gave me cues that additional people and space were a necessity. Looking past all the glitter and positivity, I locked in on what interested me the most: How were people doing, and what level of health would I encounter?

I had anticipated working with a leadership team of a half dozen. Chris considered himself to be a Christian and was excited for me to know that most of his core leadership team were also. I didn't know much more about them other than that a number of them (including Chris) had graduated a few years prior from a Christian university in the Pacific Northwest. They were attempting to apply their various degrees to earning a living, all while having fun. I was eager to see how these talented, innovative, and driven young pros were facing the demands of a start-up in a completely secular marketplace. I was intrigued by how their commitment to Jesus might be evident in the values of their company and in their day-to-day interactions, systems, and vision.

> Wholehearted Leaders stay humble and recognize that accomplishments result from God's power and the contributions of others along the way.

During our walk through the hallways, I was introduced to James and Bob, two seasoned leaders in their late fifties. Chris hired them for their experience in business, technology, and, in James's case, leading and supporting people. As we all made our way into the conference room, I noticed multiple conversations happening at once, at high volume, and just about everyone looked as if he or she had been living on a diet of energy drinks—everyone except Bob. He arrived quietly, took his seat, and was clearly keeping to himself. In contrast, James matched his younger counterparts step for step in energy and in the verbal exchange. Sometimes groups of people can embody arrogance in their exclusion of someone who doesn't fit within the majority's way of doing, learning, or communicating.

THE ROLE OF ASSESSMENTS

Prior to that day, I had asked this group to take an assessment we like to use in our counseling, coaching, and organizational development work called the Core Values Index (CVI). Created by Lynn Taylor, the CVI is a powerful tool that helps people understand their own unchanging, hardwired nature (the motivations and reasons behind what they do) and the wiring of others. With a 97 percent retest reliability, nothing else comes close in terms of getting underneath people's personalities (which can change) and their circumstances (both highs and lows) to their core nature. With the CVI, we've found that people can quickly see themselves and others more accurately and as a result are more motivated to integrate the memorable and practical key concepts into their daily lives at work, at home, or wherever else they engage.

We have implemented the CVI in counseling thousands of people: CEOs and their leadership teams (in just about every industry), married couples, families, and more. The CVI honors the complexity and nuance of every human being by transcending age, gender, and culture, and it recognizes that just as no two people have the same fingerprints, no two people communicate, learn, or engage in conflict the same way. From our vantage point, no tool compares to the CVI in helping people live more authentically and have a positive impact on the relationships they care about. So much of the wisdom gleaned from this tool is simple and practical and can be applied in real-time in any relationship. In fact, others do not have to know anything about it to directly benefit from one informed person applying its wisdom in the office, the home, the grocery store—wherever and with whomever.

Before we return to the boardroom with Chris and company, I want to explain a few things about the CVI and specifically how I was using it that day. The foundational premise of the instrument is

that we are each born with a unique set of core values th
change over time. These core values are either supported (healthy)
or rejected (unhealthy or abusive) throughout our lives. Healthy
environments develop our core values, allowing us to live out who
we are. We thrive and feel alive when this is happening. Unhealthy
environments can suppress our core values, forcing us to suppress
them as well at our own expense and the expense of others. This
is why we hate feeling stuck and want to get free. **By staying in
environments that do not welcome our core values or that force
us to suppress them to survive, we become compartmentalized
and disconnected from our potential.**

As we've stated previously, our families of origin profoundly
impact our inner-emotional health and well-being through our unique
set of unchanging core values. Every child looks to be seen and known
by their parents in alignment with his or her own core values, yet most
parents point their children in the direction of their own core values
(unintentionally). The temptation for a child to be someone he or she
is not wired to be in order to receive love, attention, and affirmation,
especially from dad and mom, is understandable. (As I write this, I
realize you may be relating in a deep way and this discussion may be
triggering something beneath the surface from your own childhood or
the way you are parenting your children.)

In the boardroom with the leadership team, I started unpacking
the four primary core values of Builder (power), Merchant (love),
Banker (knowledge), and Innovator (wisdom): their definitions and
how they influence one another. Every person has some level of each
of the four core values hardwired in him or her from birth until
death. These don't change. The lower the number associated with

a particular core value, the less likely a person will resonate with its attributes, and the higher the number of a core value, the more he or she will relate to them. The numbers for each value give the CVI nuance, helping explain and support each person's uniqueness and complexity.

Bob assessed as a Builder-Banker with a relatively strong Innovator score and lower Merchant score. He was likely wired from birth to be a highly practical and cognitive person. He exhibited a passion for information, details, facts, and fairness (the Banker's lens for seeing and interacting with the world) and was keeping to himself. Knowing Bob's wiring gave insights that I would need to pay attention to if I were to help this team operate on all cylinders. However, Chris pushed back any time I tried to integrate Bob's perspective.

Every other team member in the room was either a Merchant or an Innovator first. It quickly became clear what it might have been like for Bob as a member of this leadership team and a stakeholder in the company. In fact, Bob was twenty years Chris's senior and had been around the block. Chris, the CEO, thought it would be humorous to point out to everyone in the room, using a bit of sarcasm, that Bob was "different than the rest." This subtle posturing was a sign of Chris's arrogance, and I took note. Not willing to see anyone misuse the power of this tool (because you can, and it's never good), I made a point to follow Chris's statement with an edification of Bob. It went something like "Actually, it's Bob's core values of Banker and Builder that are likely helping this company achieve any level of success. Bob, I don't know anything about you personally, and we've never met until today. But I am willing to bet based on your test results that you're working here because you believe you can help this group complete their ideas and passions with your commitment to details, quality, facts, logic (Banker), and horsepower (Builder). They likely could not do any of their work to a high standard of excellence without you." I asked him, in front of the group, whether that resonated with him at all. In one of the few times Bob spoke in the meeting, he said "Thank you." Chris and the rest of the group softened their tone for a moment or two but then quickly returned to business as usual: loud, interrupting, bantering, and laughing.

We began to integrate the wisdom of the CVI as a platform to build trust by discussing what they were noticing about themselves and one another. By the end of the four hours, Chris and his team had made some significant headway in recognizing their contributions. As is always the case with the CVI, people have to personally commit to practicing what they know to be true and good. As I encouraged the group to integrate what they had learned about the CVI into their life and work rhythms, I left that day with hope. I knew some more observation, dialogue, and correspondence would be needed in order to coach some individuals up to their potential.

I went back the following week and made a point to meet with Chris, then Bob, and finally James. One-on-one time with these three would either validate my initial impressions and concerns about the power dynamic or provide new data that would get me closer to addressing the needs of this team. Chris welcomed me into his office. We sat down and started discussing how he wanted me to help him and his company. Chris kept the conversation on the surface. He shared about the company's origins, how they had arrived where they were today, and many of the important decisions he was making for the future. When it came to important decisions, Chris explained that only he was capable of making such decisions for the company. This immediately set off alarms, as his vision was short term and his decision-making was based on only his own perspective. Over time I learned they were growing so quickly that all their energy was invested in the here and now at the expense of quality strategic planning and execution of well-designed road maps. They were not on a path of sustainable growth.

During our scheduled one-hour meeting that Chris whittled down to thirty minutes, he controlled our interaction and made sure it was short, to the point, and on his terms. He was overtly positive and a little too optimistic as he described the confidence he had in what they were doing at the company. My impression was that he really believed that people needed *his* ideas and products. Chris believed that he was the smartest person in the company and that if he and his company didn't deliver, then the world wouldn't have what it needed. He expressed a strong desire for Bob in particular to get the message loud and clear. Chris's perspective was that Bob was a downer with a pessimistic attitude who said no too much. Chris didn't think he needed others' feedback or insights to influence his outlook, especially not Bob's.

I had hoped Chris would be the kind of servant-leader who was actually walking the talk, but in our times together it became clearer that his integrity gap was wider than he believed, even though others could see it from a mile away. Chris's overconfidence and enthusiasm about challenges reminded me of Teddy Roosevelt and his epic quest to be the first to chart the infamous River of Doubt, a tributary of the Amazon. His need to find the next thing to conquer would be to his detriment. Roosevelt rallied a team of adventurers, but at nearly every step of this one-thousand-mile expedition, he did not rely on the right people to accomplish necessary tasks. Caring only about his own vision, he dismissed the other people on his adventure until they were in life-and-death situations. Roosevelt barely survived malaria and near starvation and suffered the loss of several men.[2] Similar to many other leaders, Chris and Roosevelt were both set on a mission and refused to pay attention to the needs of their crews along the way—an arrogant mistake that led to their own demise.

After my meeting with Chris, I walked down the hall to spend some time with Bob and find out what had led him to this type of company and what he was experiencing. After a bit of history and going into a couple of things that Bob felt positive and excited about, I asked him to share about the interaction in the boardroom. He acknowledged that what had been said there and the way it made him feel was the norm in the company, but he felt the need for a more professional culture in order to sustain the company. He indicated that he had tried to be a voice of reason, but he had little confidence in Chris and the leadership team taking him or his concerns seriously.

Chris's conviction that he was the smartest person in the room resulted in a company built on a glass-castle core belief. He held—and wanted others to hold—the belief that he knew what he was doing (100 percent of the time), whether in one-on-one meetings where he enforced compliance with his adult temper tantrums or in the daily rituals and rhythms of work within the company. He isolated himself in order to make decisions and then abruptly announced them without warning, forcing direction changes and even nullifying costly work. Decisions made in isolation are often a key concern.

I told Bob it would be wise for Chris and the others to learn to rely more on his knowledge and wisdom to achieve the results they all desired. Bob shared that the process of affirming his contribution was helpful to him. It's a profound thing to witness another person feeling known after normally being deprived of such a feeling. Depending on how long it's been since someone felt acceptance, the behaviors associated with trying to get that need met may intensify or diminish. To ensure Bob felt I accurately heard the things he shared with me, I repeated them back. By mirroring, I validated those thoughts and feelings in a way that made him feel understood, heard, and not crazy for having them.

SHRINKING THIS GAP

How important is it for someone to feel heard? The brain sends a warning to the entire body, creating an alert and reactive stance (commonly known as fight, flight, or freeze) for whatever is to come when it senses danger. If a person consistently perceives possible harm (emotional, physical, or mental), he or she will live with a heightened sense of stress. In his 1995 book *Emotional Intelligence: Why It Can Matter More Than IQ*, Daniel Goleman described a neural hijacking, which is a person's triggered emotional response that is immediate, overwhelming, and out of proportion to the actual stimulus.[3]

An important voice in the field of neuroscience is Dr. Daniel Siegel, who coined the phrase *interpersonal neurobiology*. Siegel explained that through mindsight, we can focus our attention on the nature of the internal world.[4] When we focus on our own thoughts and feelings and those of others, our brains can actually

be restructured. Neuroscience has shown that we can grow pow‹
neural connections throughout our lives as we become more aware
of our own thoughts, needs, and emotions.[5]

> Recognizing a need for others is vital for any leader to stay grounded and whole.

When someone is seen, heard, and understood, that person's
brain chemistry literally changes and our bodies begin to calm
down.[6] This calming in the brain reminds the entire body that it is
safe and can return to rest. The process of mirroring, validating, and
then empathizing with a person's perspective is a powerful way to
engage this healing process at work and at home (anywhere really).
We'll speak more on effective listening in the next chapter.

Because of my own protection modes and lack of understanding, I used to think that validation was for "those" weaker people.
When Terra first shared the purpose of validation with me, as most
therapists in training try to enlighten their spouses, her interpretation intrigued me. Validation has nothing to do with me or agreeing
with another person's perspective. Validation is about putting on
another person's "glasses" to see how that person might have arrived
at his or her conclusions. This understanding was a game changer for
me. Out of a desire to live with growing authenticity and integrity,
I used to withhold validation from people who shared an opinion
different from mine. I erred on the side of honesty. Once freed from
my inaccurate definition, I started validating people all around me!

The Core Values Index helps us build an effective framework for validating and affirming others' ways of seeing the world. By appealing to people's core values, we assume the best about them and recognize who they are regardless of differing opinions, backgrounds, or expertise. Using the CVI to see people's contributions may actually help them calm down inside and out and even return to the best of who God wired them to be. We can find power, wisdom, and joy in being people who understand and value more than just our own corner of the market.

Our conversation that day in Bob's office was a shift; he felt heard and understood in a way he had not previously experienced in that environment. Bob didn't ask me to mirror, validate, or empathize with him through active listening, but he obviously hungered for that kind of response after more than a year of feeling invisible to and ignored by his teammates. As humans, we have the fundamental need for others to accurately hear, validate, and empathize with us from birth through adulthood. While coaching this company, my goal was to help develop a culture where the team could tap into Bob's Builder-Banker wiring and where he could more effectively lean into his teammates' unique contributions.

Bob had tried to articulate the reasons for his concerns and constructive criticism, but Chris, the leader at the top, would not hear them. He set the tone for the others on the leadership team. Bob needed an ally in power, but unfortunately, he was alone on this leadership team, which increased the difficulty of working within this organization. Although there were more opportunities for on-site development at this company, the bubble eventually popped (as Bob had suspected it would). After five years of business, Chris posted the classic social media announcement that the company was closing its doors and that he would be pursuing new and exciting ventures.

I wondered what might have happened with this leadership team and their budding company had Chris realized his need for more humility and awareness of others. This kind of humility has confidence that is regulated by and submitted to the influence of others to not miss their contributions for the greater good. **The reality is that sometimes leaders learn the value of humility sooner, sometimes they learn later, and sometimes they never learn.** We miss out on the opportunity to build trusted relationships and healthy interdependence with others when we believe we are the only one who knows what's best and then reinforce that over and over with our coworkers, spouse, or friends. Recognizing a need for others is vital for any leader to stay grounded and whole.

IN THE BIBLE

Leaning into others in healthy ways honors ourselves and them and is a profound sign of integrated leadership. The CVI dovetails with our highest calling as followers of Jesus to love God and others as ourselves or as God loves us (see Matt. 22:36–40; John 13:34). God designed us for relationship so that we can be rightly related to Him and mature as we learn to be rightly related to one another. And He created relationships because we need one another in order to see Him more accurately and become more like Him. If you consider yourself a follower of Jesus but are not experiencing some form of church where two or more are gathered in His name (see Matt. 18:20), you're fooling yourself in thinking that you are experiencing the fullness of God.

In parenting, we often train up our kids in the way *we would go*, counter to Proverbs 22:6: "Start children off on the way *they should go*, and even when they are old they will not turn from it" (emphasis added). In fact, the Hebrew in which this verse was written might more accurately be translated, "Start children off on the way *they are bent*, and they will not turn from it." Whether a parent, a pastor, or a CEO, leading people in light of their wiring is not only an important value to help a leader stay grounded in his or her own humanity, but it also allows for a variety of voices in the room. This means allowing others to influence us and help us stay humble. This means living out a mission or vision together.

OUR STORY

There are milestones in life that we eagerly set out to conquer with no idea of what lies ahead. Some might remember their freshman year of college, leaving home and being placed with a new roommate to share a twelve-by-eighteen-foot dorm room for a whole year. Or if you're married, you remember what it was like to begin living together and peacefully blending all the unwritten rules and unspoken expectations crafted in your childhood homes. Being open to the variety of ways and needs of others is a vital ingredient of healthy leadership and relationships.

(Terra) Our very first marital "conflict" was over my bobby pins. Growing up with a sister and then spending my young-adult years living with other female roommates, I never had *any* concern about my bobby pin habits—until I married Jeff. In our first year of marriage, as a Builder he was certain there was a place for bobby pins. He even made a special drawer where all the bobby pins could live. As a Merchant-Innovator, I was more concerned about our relationship and building a life together than the practical point of where my bobby pins landed at the end of the day. I told him he was being unloving every time he pointed out a bobby pin he found in our apartment, and he told me I was being disrespectful every time I left one anywhere but where it belonged … in the drawer. We each thought our way was best.

> He provides the resources we need not just to survive this life in isolation but actually thrive in relationship with Him and one another.

We all have these types of fights in our relationships. The kind that are on "repeat" regardless of the subject. The bottom line was we were not considering how our way was affecting the other. I soon realized that if I really cared about our relationship, I would prioritize Jeff's concern. Jeff realized that he was wasting his energy by trying to put a creative type into a structured and practical box. In the end, we both made an effort and moved toward kindness and grace. That was the last time we talked about bobby pins in almost twenty years!

The awesome thing about God's design is that He created us in the image of His triune being (Father, Son, and Holy Spirit) and uniquely hardwired each of us. He knew it would be hard for His children to navigate the challenges that exist when two or more people gather. Whether the relationship is professional, marital, familial, or social, we work well together when we find a way to learn who we are and who others are. God did not create us and then abandon us to figure out relationships on our own. In fact, He enters into every part of our relationships when we invite Him in. He provides the resources we need not just to survive this life in isolation but actually thrive in relationship with Him and one another. In His sovereign wisdom, God calls us to submit to committed relationships with Him and one another to counter our bent toward wanting things our way and thus missing the greater view. **God is so incredible that even when we are unfaithful to covenants we make with Him and others, He remains faithful to His promises to us!**

THE CALL

Learning to see the world from another's point of view is not easy, especially when we did not practice this in our homes growing up. Every single relationship provides us with an opportunity for growth. Our desire is to see healthier communities at home, at work, and at church and to develop deeper relationships of trust as we honor the core values of others. We also desire to see environments of grace where we agree, believe, and live out the reality that we can contribute while leaving room for others at the table to have a say. Whether we are shaped as action and results (Builders), relationships and vision (Merchants), assessments and solutions (Innovators), or knowledge and information (Bankers), our greatest contributions should benefit a community rather than take away from it through self-interest. The best decisions are made when all four core values are present and contributing!

As leaders, we must recognize the tendency in all of us to believe we are the most gifted and skilled in the room. When given power, do we puff ourselves up or do we breathe life into others? **Leaders of integrity benefit everyone in their wake.** Only God perfectly meets the needs of His entire team (His creation). Yet His "power is made perfect in weakness" (2 Cor. 12:9) when we humble ourselves and allow others to help us see the greater picture outside ourselves. As we practically honor our core values, which He created in us with purpose, and simultaneously commit to honoring the core values He created in others, who also bear His likeness, we become more like Him in our leadership.

Key Markers of Arrogance

- You believe you are the smartest and greatest in the room. You mock other ways of doing things, even thinking they are less Christlike.
- You know what you are doing and need little to no feedback from others.
- You use anger, annoyance, and body language (aka adult temper tantrums) to manipulate others.
- You self-isolate to make decisions and then spontaneously tell others the plan.
- You change direction and expectations regularly without considering other perspectives, even nullifying costly work.
- You are preoccupied with being seen and heard.
- You fail to see or value the contributions others are wired to make, which are likely to create better outcomes.

Antidotes

1. What did your family relationships model to you about needs, teamwork, and asking for help? Reflect on patterns you were exposed to in your childhood.

2. If you have never taken it, check out the Core Values Index. Go to www.livingwholehearted.com, and take the assessment to discern your own core values. Have at least one other person also take the CVI, and then unpack the results. (This person can be a friend, a spouse, or a trusted colleague.)

3. Whom do you invite to share feedback with you? What characteristics must someone have for you to trust that person's input on your most important endeavors? How do you avoid isolating and making decisions without the influence of others?

4. Which other core value type (Merchant, Banker, Builder, Innovator) is the hardest for you to understand or empathize with?

5. Consider doing a word study in the Bible on humility, the antidote to arrogance, and see what God does when you prayerfully ask Him to grow this virtue in you.

Chapter 8

BLIND SPOTS

Too Little Time to Listen

*Leaders who refuse to listen will eventually be surrounded
by people who have nothing significant to say.*
—Andy Stanley

Wholehearted Leaders are aware of their influence in the room. They see others for who they are and consider their wiring, their context, and their sense of power. These leaders focus on seeing each person before them and not allowing themselves to be alienated by that person's style of communication or sense of entitlement or shame. Jesus models how to listen well to all types of followers, and a Wholehearted Leader follows in His footsteps.

(Jeff) Between Christmas Day and New Year's Day each year, I reflect on the closing year and the new one that is quickly approaching. A number of years ago, I decided it would be a good idea to have a permanent resolution on my list: *become a better listener.* Thinking back to the family I grew up in and my first lessons in communication, I realize we were better at talking than listening. It was a challenge then and is a challenge now (with my own wife and kids) to not interrupt, talk over each other, or have more than one conversation going at once! In our family today, we are working to remember what Alfred Brendel said: "The word 'listen' contains the same letters as the word 'silent.'"[1] We know it is vitally important for us to be engaged in listening to our girls—and to anyone else we interact with in order to reap the benefits of an engaged focus. It's an art to listen well.

> Effective listening is essential to being known, integrating our whole selves, building trust, developing intimacy, promoting efficiency, and more!

Why is good listening such a critical skill to develop? Well, *consider the cost of the alternative.* Do you know any couples who have a long-term thriving marriage but don't listen to each other? Good luck finding any! Parents know from mountains of research that children feel most loved and emotionally secure in their formative years when parents engage in listening to them. Friendships start to experience wear and tear when conversations feel lopsided over the years. Effective listening is more than a New Year's resolution. Effective listening is essential to being known, integrating our whole selves, building trust, developing intimacy, promoting efficiency, and more! Consider the wisdom of a nursery rhyme that John Wooden (considered to be the greatest coach of all time) learned when he was a boy:

A wise old owl sat in an oak.

The more he heard the less he spoke.

The less he spoke, the more he heard.

The more he heard, the more he learned.

Now wasn't he a wise old bird?[2]

Failure to listen well is an integrity gap that comes in many shapes and sizes, so our communication skills are another area for us all to consider. Each of the four core value types are uniquely wired for communicating, so Wholehearted Leaders will want to understand these differences to reduce misunderstandings and inefficiency.

EFFECTIVE LISTENING

How do we ensure people feel safe and heard in our homes, workplaces, and communities, especially when we all have a pull toward thinking our way is the best way? Effective listening is the path to keeping ourselves from becoming arrogant and dismissing the value of others in our lives. Here are some basic descriptions of effective listening tools that anyone can learn to use:

- Mirroring is reflecting back what a person is saying. This is not a time for interpretation, and no questions should be asked until the person is completely done sharing. Oftentimes questions can dominate and control a conversation, so any clarifying questions are asked only after the speaker has finished sharing.

• Validating is putting on the lens of someone else and using a nonjudgmental approach to meet that person where he or she is. Validating is not agreeing with the other person, but in humility seeing someone else's viewpoint and letting them know you can. This practice is especially important with our children when we might be tempted to doubt the validity of their perspectives. Validation shows respect for and acknowledges another's point of view.

• Empathizing is the final—and often missed—step in effective listening. Less about cerebral understanding, it is where human attachment, connection, and comfort grow and we receive the message *I am not alone.* We often skip this last step, thinking that emotions are not as significant a factor. However, empathizing is the most powerful means of changing our way of interacting.[3]

IMPROVING LISTENING THROUGH THE CVI

We love how the Core Values Index helps us in so many practical ways, including the art of listening. Each of the four core value types (Merchants, Innovators, Bankers, and Builders) have a unique communication style. Imagine if you were adept at understanding how others were wired to communicate and then you delivered your message in the ways they were most likely to receive it. This method works everywhere we engage with people: in leadership teams, with direct reports, in marriage, and with our children and teenagers— truly, it applies everywhere. The challenge, of course, is the comical way we as humans expect that others will prefer to give and receive communications the way we do!

Each core value type has a unique communication process and conflict strategy that can easily run interference. After learning more about the CVI with us, a friend of ours put it this way: **Builders are the action people, Merchants are the people people, Innovators are the options people, and Bankers are the detail people.**[4]

	BUILDERS	MERCHANTS
	ACTION PEOPLE	PEOPLE PEOPLE
	DETAIL PEOPLE	OPTIONS PEOPLE
	BANKERS	INNOVATORS

Understanding each core value's communication style is incredibly valuable. Because you can be operating from only one core value at a time, your communication style at a given moment will reveal what that core value is. It's helpful to know what is needed in the conversation on the delivery end (how to communicate with someone based on that person's present core value) and on the receiving end (how you are expecting communication to come to you based on your present core value). **When we make efforts to honor the core values of others, we are practically living out the Golden Rule: "Do to others as you would have them do to you" (Luke 6:31).** The fun part is when they start trying to honor your core values too!

Merchants

Possessing the most relational wiring type, Merchants use an emotional, roundabout way of communicating. Their love of and need for interacting with people on a regular basis makes them very comfortable verbally processing with others. In fact, talking and listening to others is not just fun for Merchants; it is like oxygen, helping them learn and gain clarity about themselves and others. On the flip side, if they're deprived of regular communication, they will eventually explode verbally or find their internal world confused and emotionally toxic. For Merchants, talking with others *is the point*. They are often the best storytellers, and they can help the community emote, connect, and network and can smooth over awkward transitions with their words. The diagram below will help you understand and remember *how* a Merchant processes.

MERCHANT

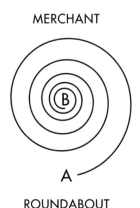

ROUNDABOUT

When Merchants have a topic to discuss, whether it's as simple as what might be good for dinner or as serious as a critical health treatment decision, they start at point A but soon veer off course (at least it seems that way to those with much lower Merchant scores). The spiral is representative of the roundabout way Merchants arrive at B (their main point), which is the clarity they were seeking about A to begin with. Here's the wild part: it is not uncommon for a Merchant to arrive at B without the listening party ever saying a word! (Terra and I share Merchant as our strongest common core value, and when we announce, "I am in Merchant mode," the other knows to hang on and enjoy the ride.)

The roundabout style of Merchants is their God-designed way to get to their B, whatever it is. We honor Merchants when we can be present and track with them. These are good questions to ask yourself when trying to hang with a Merchant who is processing out loud: *Is this his A? Is he on the spiral? Is he getting closer to his B? Has he gotten to B yet?* If you can consider these clarifying questions without sounding frustrated, feel free to ask the Merchant if you are lost or are uncertain where you are right now. If you check out, cut him off, or decide to fact-check him in a condescending manner, a Merchant may move into his conflict strategy of manipulation, using words to harm and maneuvering to get his emotional needs met in an unhealthy way.

If you are primarily a Merchant and realize you are wanting or needing to verbally process with someone, let the other person know with a clear disclaimer: "I am in Merchant mind-set and am not drawing conclusions or making decisions. I am only needing a listening ear to help me make sense of what I think and feel inside. Are you able to process with me at this time?" A Builder, Innovator, or Banker can set herself up for success in a conversation like this by informing the Merchant of how much time she can in good faith give and asking whether this would be enough to help. If the Merchant says that amount of time is all he thinks he needs, then both parties can feel honored. If the Merchant is needing more time than the listener can offer, scheduling the conversation is wise and freeing for both parties (as long as there is follow-through).

This strategy works in most relationships, especially marriages. In fact, Merchants need a few options to go to in case their main person is not emotionally or physically available. Journaling is a great backup, but in the end a person is still necessary for a Merchant to feel at rest and to arrive at B. On the other side, if you notice someone wanting to verbally process something with you, ask her whether that's what she's seeking. If so, let her do most of the talking as she passionately pursues her B.

Innovators

Being so good at assessing and solving problems, Innovators prefer to communicate with complexity rather than drawing quick conclusions or having just one B. Unique attributes of Innovators are that they value wisdom and see the world in shades of gray. They use the data they have collected from personal experience, Bankers' research, and others' mistakes to connect missing links. Innovators do not often see clear-cut answers, but they do believe there is a right and best way to do things. They hold deep and messy complexity well, which can feel heavy to the other core values.

When Innovators discern that a situation is going to require more time to assess, they commit to doing that and wait to identify the best solution among all the options (all the Bs) before acting. Knowing this about Innovators helps non-Innovator types understand why they ask so many clarifying questions, regularly offer alternate ideas (even after a decision has been made), or seem like they are not fully present. Innovators are assessing and solving—sometimes out loud—but most often in their heads.

Innovators have what some might think of as a superpower. You see it when two strong Innovators are talking. They might not use complete sentences, or they might finish each other's sentences. Terra is wired like this, and I have witnessed her and other Innovator friends (male or female) do this. To honor Innovators' communication style, see their wisdom and get their input on problems you're trying to solve. Be mindful not to minimize the complexity they so easily see or push them to action before they have had time to assess and work through the process. Innovators' conflict strategy is interrogation. Instead of offering help, they will try to complicate the situation and belittle in order to get their listeners to hear their wisdom. The diagram below will help you understand and remember the process Innovators use to learn, relate to others, and gain the clarity they seek.

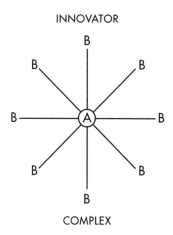

INNOVATOR

COMPLEX

In the diagram, A is the starting point of the topic being discussed. Immediately an Innovator sees many variables (Bs) that each relate in some way to A. The assessing has begun and can take moments or days, depending on whether the Innovator evaluates based on his wisdom or believes he needs to dig into more data for the right solution. One of the important lessons we've learned through applying the CVI is that Terra will *always* see many more Bs than I will. I can get locked in on one or two Bs (solutions) and think those are all we're discussing at the moment. Wrong! I have learned to ask Terra (before the conversation ends) if she has more Bs we need to discuss before making a decision or concluding a discussion. Terra has also learned to prioritize the Bs she needs to discuss and to recognize when a B does not need to be shared. For an Innovator, this requires energy, forethought, and consideration of others, and it involves just as much energy for a listener. We both win when we do this process well. We both lose when we think our way of communicating is the best way.

Bankers

Wired to value knowledge, facts, and excellence in all things, Bankers prefer to communicate in great detail and in a linear fashion. They have an insatiable appetite for reading and analyzing information, and they can retain that knowledge better than the other types. Like Merchants, Bankers are people persons who have a strong commitment to relationships, but they approach relationships from a different perspective. One of their greatest contributions is that Bankers care about people having the resources they need. Bankers' critical eye and resulting comments about what's broken or needs more attention are coming from their wiring—their desire to use their knowledge, sense of justice, and commitment to excellence in order to help the rest of the core value types thrive. At their healthiest, Bankers want improvement only so people can be equipped.

If Bankers' contributions are not welcomed or honored in a system (home, work, church community), they quickly get discouraged and move to their conflict strategy of aloof judgment. The critical eye once focused on helping the community now sees you as guilty. When someone who scores high as a Banker starts to withdraw or go silent, "the most important thing in communication is to hear what isn't being said."[5] We honor Bankers by asking them in advance to contribute knowledge, facts, and prudent courses of action after reading and analyzing. Bankers do not like being put on the spot; give them time to gather their thoughts (and paperwork), and they are most likely going to bring their best to the table. When a Banker is trying to communicate, it's likely to look something like the diagram below.

BANKER

A ★★★★★★★★★★★★★★★★★★★★★★★★★★ B

DETAILED

Though Bankers start with A, their journey to B is more of a report than a process of discovery. Bankers relate how each point or detail leads to the next point until they finally arrive at B. Although it can be challenging for the other core value types to listen well to the Bankers in their lives, they are likely to benefit if they can learn to be mindful of the why and how of a Banker's communication style.

Affirming Bankers for their desire to help people have what they need, acknowledging that there are important facts that are valuable to communicate, and asking them to gather more data (in advance of needing it) are all relational deposits one can make with higher Bankers. In fact, we have learned that Bankers are some of the most thoughtful people because they pay close attention to details. If you say you like a specific brand of ice cream, you bet you just might get that delivered to your door on your birthday. As long as there are not too many withdrawals from the relationship at their expense, Bankers are wired to want to do things well. In fact, they may mirror what you share better than you could have said it. They know you're working through a unique process to arrive at B. When they are at their best, Bankers apply the information they learn about each wiring well.

Builders

Action and results oriented at their core, Builders prefer to communicate in a to-the-point manner, sharing only what is necessary to get the action and results they seek. Be careful not to misjudge their typical brevity as rudeness or coldheartedness. Builders are direct communicators because they're always trying to do something to make a *positive difference* in their relationships and communities. Even if you think you've caught them doing nothing, Builders are actually doing something! Even resting is intentional. The diagram below reveals the way Builders prefer to give and receive communication. A is the starting point, with as short a distance between A and B as possible.

BUILDER

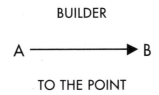

TO THE POINT

Sitting in a committee meeting discussing ideas, an organization's vision, or spreadsheets can be a nightmare for Builders. To have the best chance of being heard and understood by a Builder, it's critical to condense your thoughts—put requests or wordy communication into small chunks with as few words as possible. We honor Builders when we ask them to help by completing meaningful projects, especially when they are given freedom and trusted to get the projects done by themselves. They are more likely to do likewise, learning to include others before they finish their projects, tapping Merchants for vision, Innovators for wise strategies, and Bankers for precise excellence.

When Builders' efforts are being challenged or their competency to execute is questioned, Builders default to a conflict strategy of intimidation. Now instead of using their strength to build with the good of all in mind, they feel a need to move people and obstacles out of their way to get things done. It's usually pretty intense, harsh, and aimed to win at the expense of others.

SHRINKING THIS GAP

Our ability to listen well is impacted by the differences in our wiring. When contemplating how to shrink the gap in communication blind spots, consider paying closer attention to the cues people give when they talk to you. Even without knowing their official CVI scores, you are likely to discern how they prefer to give and receive communication. If it's in a roundabout manner, consider whether you have the time to let them verbally process with you. If it's more complex with a lot of Bs that do not always seem connected, let them share those Bs and then ask whether there are more before moving on. If they communicate in a more detailed, slow, and methodical manner, give them uninterrupted time to speak, and understand where they are. How we communicate with and listen to those we lead in our homes and in our work spaces reflects our integrity.

IN THE BIBLE

Stories in the Bible display many ways of communicating, some more effective than others. Jesus models wholehearted leadership, exhibiting patience when interrupted, tuning in to various communication styles, and listening well. When we meet Him in Mark 5, Jesus is busy calming a storm, preaching, and healing the sick. You can imagine His weariness as He got out of the boat after traveling across the lake. One of the synagogue leaders, Jairus, came directly up to Jesus and fell at His feet. He pleaded with Jesus to help his dying daughter by coming to his house to lay His healing hands on her. Jairus was used to being in charge, and as a leader, he had the privilege of walking up to anyone. He might have been a Builder who was taking action and being to the point with Jesus.

"Come. My daughter needs healing." Verse 24 says, "So Jesus went with him." Jesus didn't get offended by Jairus's bold directness. He could see the heart behind the request and was ready to jump into action with him.

Time was ticking as Jesus and Jairus moved through the large crowd that pressed against them. Among the people was a woman who had been sick for twelve years. In her Jewish culture, she was the opposite of Jairus—considered unclean and untouchable because of her never-ending bleeding (menstruation). This woman had spent all she had on care from doctors and was also desperate for healing. She saw her last chance, but instead of going right to Jesus, she came from behind and touched His cloak. She thought, "If I just touch his clothes, I will be healed" (v. 28).

When she touched Jesus, she was instantly healed and freed from her suffering. Jesus turned and asked, "Who touched my clothes?" (v. 30). The woman fell at His feet and told Him her story. Even though Jairus was panicking as his child was dying at home, Jesus took the time to look this woman in the eyes. He listened to her whole truth—every word. He then said to her, "Daughter, your faith has healed you. Go in peace and be freed from your suffering" (v. 34). This suffering was the shame that told her she was marginalized and unacceptable. Jesus called her "daughter," giving her identity and belonging with His spoken word before moving on to the next task at hand. It was not enough to just heal her physically. He also healed her emotionally—from her shame at being unseen and unheard for twelve long years. He then made it to Jairus's home, where they found his daughter already dead. The family was angry because Jesus was not "on time." But Jesus took the twelve-year-old girl's hand and healed her. "Get up!" (v. 41).

> Jesus models wholehearted leadership, exhibiting patience when interrupted, tuning in to various communication styles, and listening well.

Jesus was interrupted by two people in need yet took time to lean in and hear their needs. So often, whether leading in our homes or in our organizations, we move too quickly in the flow of our own agendas. We get caught up in protocols detailing how people are supposed to approach us. Though Jesus was robbed of time, Jairus, as a church leader, needed to see how He looked this outcast woman in the eyes. Even touching her. The woman's cautious approach of touching Jesus from behind must have resulted from years and years of being told "You do not matter." Whether it was her natural communication style from her family of origin or dictated by cultural norms, touching Jesus' hem was all she could do. Jesus was tuned in and saw her. In contrast, Jairus's communication style and background taught him to march in and ask for what he needed. No fluff. He needed Jesus, and Jesus acted, although He didn't do so on Jairus's timetable. Jesus was making a point there too.

Being a listening, responsive leader is not just about mirroring, validating, and empathizing. It might also be about being interrupted. To lead like Jesus often requires more time with and exposure to our followers than we are willing to give. It means humility and growing to value people, not just their words and how they help us get to our destinations. Jesus models a kind of leadership that flips protocol on its head; He makes it a priority to affirm, value, and hear from others. He sees the heart. Leading well simply means listening well.

Key Markers of Blind Spots

- You feel impatience with the way people communicate, and interruptions are your greatest pet peeve.
- You let tasks take priority over people.
- You think you understand what people are saying, but they feel unheard.
- You have little or no time to hear the heart of a matter.
- You rarely allow time or ask for feedback, especially about your influence of others or your leadership. If given feedback, you quickly dismiss it.

Antidotes

1. Study the active listening skills: mirror, validate, and empathize. Intentionally practice these in your home or with those you lead, and notice the impact on those relationships. Watch for a transformation in their body language and response to you as an influencer in their lives.

2. Pause and consider two or three people in your life: your kids, your spouse, your colleagues, your board members, or your team

members. Who in your life might invite you into a Merchant's spiral communication style? An Innovator's complex communication style? A Banker's detailed style? A Builder's to-the-point style?

3. Practice the art of noticing how people interact with you. Do they seem afraid to approach you? Are they bold and direct? Who in your system directly asks for their needs, and who takes the back door or waits in the crowd?

4. Think about interruptions on your time and agenda. How do they make you feel? How do you handle them in real time? How could you reframe them so you stay open to greater leadership moments (keeping relationships at the forefront and not tasks)? Write your thoughts or discuss them with another person.

Chapter 9

BURNOUT

It's Easier for Me to Just Do It

*What do you benefit if you gain the whole world but lose
your own soul? Is anything worth more than your soul?*
—Matthew 16:26 NLT

Being a responsible, highly efficient leader who can power through any
stressful situation is both valuable and applauded in our culture. Yet
this kind of leading comes with a price tag: burnout. At some point
we—and those we love—pay the price. In our youth we tend to rely
more on our natural abilities, as we do not see the effects of our driven
leadership on our bodies, our minds, our relationships, and ultimately
our souls. Some of us have to train more to attain certain aspects of
leadership. Others can jump in with natural abilities. However, in
either case, the more we train, learning how to pace ourselves in the
race of leadership, the less damage we do along the way to ourselves
and those we love. Burnout is not a badge of honor but a warning sign
that we are ignoring our limits and not leaning into others.

(Terra) I ran a marathon in my early twenties. One marathon was
good enough for me. That's one more than Jeff ever did. Ironically,
Jeff's the natural runner and did track most of his life leading up to

college. At the time, I was determined to experience a runner's high at some point in my life. I thought runners were a little crazy, and I was curious how a person could run 26.2 miles and enjoy it. I did my research and found that training was the key to enjoying the race and not paying the price afterward. At one point in my training, I did the Vancouver, BC, half marathon, and Jeff decided to jump in the day of the race, after I spent months training and equipping myself for the "battle." I thought, *No fair!* However, after the race I recovered faster because I had spent time preparing my body. I was ready to keep going days later while Jeff was still recovering. Though he did the same race in a faster time, his body was paying the price of his last-minute decision. Sound familiar at all? Even in his early twenties, there was a cost to not preparing.

For close to twenty years, leaders—particularly ministry lead-ers—have shown up in our offices past the point of caring anymore. One pastor could not drive himself to the appointments, as he was having severe panic attacks and felt as if he were going to die at any moment. One woman stopped eating and felt as if she could not leave her bed for months. Her bone-tired body gave up before she realized she was done. Compassion fatigue and burnout are as real as gravity. **Leaders are humans too.** Years and years of caring for others take their toll, and one day what we believe to be secondary trauma hits the mind, body, and soul like an enormous hammer. As we ignore our smaller needs that whisper to us along the way, it takes a full-throttle meltdown to get our attention. Warning signs can be when caring seems like too much work, when another person's tragic story elicits a "Whatever" under your breath, or when bone-deep tiredness haunts every task at hand.

DEFINING THE GAP

So what's behind the tendency of leader types to believe it would be easier to take tasks on themselves, at the risk of burnout, than lean into others to get the job done? This mentality may feed the narcissistic tendencies of some. We've identified that all leaders deal with some level of narcissism. Others might have a bit of a savior or superhero complex. There's nothing wrong with achievement and being part of success; it feels good to be part of the solution and success! For leaders, it always comes down to motive: *Why am I doing this?* Those on the narcissistic personality disorder (NPD) spectrum are always hunting for opportunities to control their image in other people's minds. These predatory types of leaders have no trouble taking opportunities from others, blaming others, and controlling the narrative of the results so anything perceived as negative is distanced from them. Maybe that sounds familiar if you've borne the brunt of a self-serving leader who used you and left you hanging out to dry. It's difficult to trust leadership after an experience like that. However, the reality is that **most leaders are dealing with the lure of efficiency and control.**

> For leaders, it always comes down to motive: *Why am I doing this?*

Efficiency is "the state or quality of being ... able to accomplish something with the least waste of time and effort; competency in performance."[1] Returning to the wisdom of the CVI for a moment, for people wired as Innovators, efficiency is a key outcome of applying their wisdom. In the CVI, wisdom is "seeing the way things are and knowing what to do about it."[2] Builders are the other core value type who enjoy a high level of efficiency but in a different way. Builders want action and results. Nothing frustrates Innovators and Builders more than a waste of time, energy, or finances that could (or should) have been used elsewhere for a better return. These are just a few ways that our God-designed hardwiring can dictate our perspectives on who we are and what a leader does or does not do.

If we do not resist the temptation to pursue efficiency without letting others, especially God, help us along the way, burnout will probably be the number-one result. In her book *Strengthening the Soul of Your Leadership*, Barton told of an emerging leader who wisely said, "I feel the call of God to move deeper and deeper into service through preaching and leadership. At the same time I am keenly aware of what ministry is doing to the personal spiritual lives of almost everyone I know on staff or in key volunteer positions in the church."[3] This young leader was noticing a phenomenon, or a pattern, that can easily be corrected if we begin to collectively change our paradigms about what is healthy and normal for leaders to handle.

IN THE BIBLE

A common expectation for leaders, particularly Christian leaders such as pastors, is that the needs of those they lead are so urgent that God will sustain them beyond measure and they will find rest when they get to heaven. In fact, we have heard leaders use that as a badge of honor, saying, "I will enter the gates of heaven ready for my rest." This kind of thinking raises several questions: *Is this God's design? When we read Scripture, do we find bone-wearying leadership an honorable thing? Or is this a warning sign that we are living outside the limits of who God designed us to be and trying to take on more than we are meant to carry? In a subtle way, are we trying to become the savior rather than trusting Jesus to be the Savior?*

Matthew 11:28–30 says,

> Are you tired? Worn out? Burned out on religion? Come to me. Get away with me and you'll recover your life. I'll show you how to take a real rest. Walk with me and work with me—watch how I do it. Learn the unforced rhythms of grace. I won't lay anything heavy or ill-fitting on you. Keep company with me and you'll learn to live freely and lightly. (THE MESSAGE)

Burnout is a sign of pharisaical religious thinking. *Work harder. Try harder. Do more. Be more. God expects more of us. Look busy. Jesus is coming.* However, something about Jesus and His leadership guides us to a different way of being: Learning the unforced rhythms of grace. Taking a real rest.

Our family is part of a larger church in the suburbs of Portland, Oregon. Our lead pastor has come up through the ranks from youth pastor to executive pastor to lead pastor over the forty-plus-year history of the church. Not too long ago, he was addressing mental health and the validity of learning how to seek and receive help when needed. In this context, our pastor shared about his own burnout experience. After working with a short list of trusted resources, he learned to identify the contributing factors that led to his thoughts, patterns, and physical fatigue in that season. We desire more shepherd leaders to normalize care for mental health, as so many in the church are dealing with their own mental health concerns or those of someone they love. **When leaders do not model how to care for themselves, their followers are left feeling guilt, even shame, when they address their own needs.**

We are so grateful for the gift our pastor gave us and our community. He didn't pretend that he was immune to the challenges of being a leader. He normalized the feelings that many, if not most, leaders in the church could relate to if they were honest. It's normal to think we will have all the answers if we just keep trying. It's normal to think it's up to us to personally help solve the cares and concerns in a congregation or company. These false beliefs can lead to unhealthy behaviors, discouragement, and despair. He pointed our church family to the only Savior, Jesus, who helps us all … leaders or not. In publicly sharing his journey of overextending himself, which had led to a season of depression, our pastor demonstrated that even leaders need to rely on God's help. His vulnerability from the pulpit—recommending practical tools, rhythms, and systems he learned in his season of despair—is helping others stay healthier. He made it okay to acknowledge our own limits and risk taking off our "I am fine" masks on Sunday mornings. Sometimes, no matter how efficient or in control we think we need to be, the fruit of our lives is saying that something needs to change. We are faced with a choice to let go, delegate, or trust God with the "half-finished" work of our hands.

THE LIE

We are old enough to realize that in the past it would have been taboo for a pastor to share personal things from the pulpit. In fact, we still hear pastors and other Christian leaders defend the idea that it is inappropriate for a pastor to admit to any human weakness. We have created a system that puts leaders on pedestals, believing they are above their own humanity. Then we curse them (even discard them) when they fall off the pedestals and land flat on their faces. Something needs to change.

Eugene Peterson spoke to this issue in the book he coauthored with Marva Dawn, *The Unnecessary Pastor*: "The constant danger for those of us who enter the ranks of the ordained is that we take on a role, a professional religious role, that gradually obliterates the life of the soul."[4] Many leaders, leaning into their larger-than-average capacity to achieve and perform, find themselves believing another lie that can lead to burnout through isolation, lost opportunities, and stressed relationships. We commonly believe it would be easier to just do things ourselves rather than empower, trust, or rely on anyone else to get them done. The truth is, it's really not leadership if you are doing everything. The best leaders develop others to do work, entrusting and fostering rather than controlling and micromanaging. Similarly, if we want our children to be able to do their own laundry and be responsible adults someday (giving their spouses and budgets a break on the cost of marital therapy down the road), training our children to do chores is great leadership.

When our older daughter was twelve years old, we asked her to start doing all the dishes. At first this seemed brilliant. There would be no dishes for us parents, so more time to relax and take a deep breath after each meal. What actually took place was a process of lowering expectations of what "clean dishes" meant, spending a little extra time doing dishes with her until she got the hang of the system, and negotiating the timing of when the dishes needed to get done so that everyone was happy. Compromise was initially needed, but we have come to see her own this job. She likes getting paid for this responsibility too! Some jobs in our home aren't paid, as they just come with being part of a family. We need reminders and patience because we always feel a pull to just do it ourselves. Although her way of doing dishes is far different from ours, we've adjusted our expectations for the greater good of us all.

STORIES OF BURNOUT

This small example can be applied to the highest level of leadership in any organization. It is a common struggle to think that leading means *I have to do it all because they could not do it right and because I'm faster, and what will they think if I am not getting my hands dirty? Doesn't servant leadership mean always busting my own tail?*

(Terra) I am guilty here. In fact, the growth of our company has served as a mirror to reflect my control issues. As a marriage and family therapist for so many years, I have a passion for *how* therapy should look. But in the last ten years, I have grown in my coaching and training of other therapists, recognizing that they have their own gifts, strengths, and contributions to make to their clients. We are

only the vessels for God to use to work in the relationship at hand, as
He is the great counselor.

One day God whispered the word *cocreate* to my heart while
I attended a leadership conference. It painfully resonated with my
need for and yet fear of allowing another to influence "the way it
should go." Building a platform on one person is a dangerous model
for that person and for the mission. Our marriages and children suffer, dying on the altar of doing good, even doing ministry for God
and the greater community. Not only does empowering others give
us margin, but it also allows others to participate in a greater vision
beyond a one-man pony show. Jeff and I have never aspired to be
the kind of leaders that people follow. We want to lead people to the
greater vision of following God—who knows them and knows the
purposes He designed in them to give to the world.

> We are only the vessels for God to use
> to work in the relationship at hand, as
> He is the great counselor.

I remember sitting with a couple; the husband was the
president of a well-known *Fortune* 500 company who could kill
a thousand birds with one stone every single day. This church
elder, board chairman, and mentor to many was admired by the
community and sought after for his wisdom, expertise, and counsel. **I heard myself tell him, "Efficiency is your mistress."** He

suddenly realized why his wife had been saying she was lonely in the marriage. His success was admirable, and his wife saw it as an asset. However, neither of them could make sense of why she rarely felt close to him and often felt like his last priority. In fact, she rarely saw the ways she contributed to their lives—parenting and caring for their home, their community, and even their marriage—because he was so quick to do it all and move on to the next task. He seemed fine doing most everything by himself. Partnership was a theory he believed in but never practiced.

How did this profoundly gifted leader get to this place? In childhood he was the kid everyone was in awe of and knew was destined for great things. He genuinely loved Jesus and was committed to giving God glory for all he accomplished. He found his way in the world by performing and giving his all to any task, and he was given much power. His Core Values Index revealed both a deep need for wisdom and efficiency and a drive to get any job done well. The one missing thing was learning how to keep in touch with his humanity and the humanity of his high-performing wife and children. More than a dad on the front lines doing good for God and his community, they desperately needed him on the home front, to sit and play with them and hear about their day. This man never realized his acts of kindness were not always helpful to himself or others. I spent years helping this couple learn how to rest, cry, laugh, watch a movie, and play together and with their kids. His wife was forever grateful to find companionship in her marriage after years of thinking her duty was to support a man who contributed so much to the world around her for the sake of Christ. Slowing down can be the greatest discipline for many leaders.

> Wholehearted leadership requires a strong relationship with the One who knows who we are and why He made us.

Ruth Barton said, "These days (and maybe every day) there is real tension between what the human soul needs in order to be truly well and what life in leadership encourages and even requires. There is the tension between being and doing, community and cause, truth-telling and putting the right spin on things. There is the tension between the time it takes to love people and the need for expediency. There is the tension between the need for measurable goals and the difficulty of measuring that which is ultimately immeasurable by anyone but God himself."[5] As we mentioned in chapter 3, Barton unpacked the life of Moses, who hit real burnout. After years of living in dynamic tension—being a leader while witnessing the abusive oppression of his own people, carrying his adoption story wounds, being abandoned twice by his own mother, being disconnected from his true identity, and dealing with the demands of his role—he snapped. He became so angry he killed a man, and then he fled into the wilderness to hide his shame. He had no other place to go and forged the depths of his relationship with God in the silent places, where he faced his own inner life.

By the time he returned to leadership in older age, he had a new bent and way of being. Moses leaned on his relationship with God and listened to His instructions instead of the instructions of those around him. He lived out the long haul of leadership, modeling delegation in his leading of the Israelites rather than attempting to remain the sole judge for over 600,000 men (not including women and children).

Wholehearted leadership requires a strong relationship with the One who knows who we are and why He made us. It's easy to get lost in the demands of the day and the asks of all those in need around us. It's harder to face our stories and the depths of our own human needs than to keep going until we hit the wall. Our hair starts falling out. Our health starts deteriorating. Our friendships feel distant. Our lid keeps flipping. One day we wake up and realize we are no longer who we once were, and it feels like too much work to find ourselves again.

In any number of situations, it may be best for you to take on a challenge, especially if it taps your unique talents, voice, and skill set and no one else has a similar ability. For example, if you're the president of a large company, the board likely has empowered you to be the face and voice of the company. That's part of your role and unique contribution to the company. The research assistant in the basement, whose gifts are in the details, may not be wired to be the public face and voice of the organization. She may lack the authority, experience, and capability for the job. She may also be terrified at the thought, which is why she enjoys her cozy cube with limited interactions and interruptions. We're all wired to contribute in different ways, each equally valuable even if one person's contribution is situationally more valuable than another's.

SHRINKING THIS GAP

For leaders, putting their commitment to efficiency before others' important needs (as well as their own) can become a subtle form of idolatry. They can easily lose sight of the forest because of the trees. An example is when leaders rush into automating tasks that had previously been performed by people. In addition, the more responsibility leaders take on, the more they have to prioritize and execute. This can lead to mistrust and resentment as leaders, who are now doing others' jobs in addition to their own, aren't able to utilize their God-given strengths. Their available bandwidth shrinks, and they may find themselves more isolated and behind than they ever expected. **Isolate any living thing and it is probably dying.** People dislike being isolated for long periods of time because of our human need for connection. (We will unpack this idea in the next chapter.)

As leaders, we need to guard against the tendency to isolate ourselves while seeking efficiency. We may have good intentions. We tell ourselves it will be only for a week, and then a week turns into months. It's only for a season, and then the season turns into two years. We say we can't focus because of constant interruptions, so a rarely closed door becomes regularly closed. We don't want to face any more demanding people, so we hope they don't notice when we start working less at the office and more at home without telling anyone. Then there is the valid concern that when we invite others into the process, they will not meet our standards or get the job done. The fear of failing can plague leaders but provides an opportunity to grow trust—trust in God and trust in others, only reaffirming the need to lead by modeling. The solution is to take responsibility for their success by either mentoring people directly or finding someone who can.

As we sit with CEOs and help them process the people issues that keep them up at night, it's not uncommon to hear they've lost perspective on their ability to effect change. They can get overwhelmed or burned out and stuck in react mode. Some are in avoidance mode, even hoping that everything will somehow improve while they ignore it. At the end of the day, leaders are, as Henry Cloud said, "ridiculously in charge."[6] He told about a time he discussed people issues with an executive. He helped him realize he had the authority and power to solve the people issues, not just talk about them. Cloud said, "In the end, as a leader, you are always going to get a combination of two things: what you create and what you allow."[7]

THE CALL

As a leader, you're more responsible for issues—including your own burnout—than you may be acknowledging. By showing humility and vulnerability in addressing the issues you desire to see fixed (even if you are part of the cause), you give others permission to take responsibility for their part and find motivation to bring about positive change. That kind of leadership can generate trust, loyalty, and lasting results. "Part of a leader's job is to engage people in grappling with the tension between freedom and constraint," between "liberty and limits."[8] How will they be able to do this effectively if you don't know how? There might be something to the saying "We're better together" after all.

We long to see a shift to long-term sustainable leadership that honors the whole person, not just a person's ability to accomplish tasks and reach goals. **We want to see a culture shift toward valuing and applauding wholehearted leadership, where we trust God and others with who we are and what we do.** Though we all want to exemplify skilled leadership and tend to lean into our natural gifts, we need to contemplate developing a deeper kind of leadership that will help us all stay more in step with the leadership Jesus modeled, which is free and light.

Key Markers of Burnout

- You feel guilty when asking someone to take on a task for you, or you take on other people's tasks without any boundaries in place.
- You have no time for hobbies, playtime, or even friendships. People feel like a bother rather than a joy.
- You expend little effort or time on body care, including exercising, sleeping well, and eating well on a consistent basis.
- Your enjoyment of solitary times with God and in the Word is diminishing. Cynicism and doubt creep in more regularly.
- You feel numb. Nothing seems to affect you anymore (good or bad). You feel as if you're going through the motions and may even lack empathy and patience for family and friends.
- You feel the weight of every decision, person, and need in your wake. You may have physical symptoms: stomachaches, sleepless nights, headaches, hair loss, chest pain, back pain, etc.

Antidotes

1. Evaluate whether you have allowed the idea *"It will be easier if I just do things myself"* to consume more of your leadership ecosystem than is healthy for you or those you lead. Write out some of the messages you tell yourself under stress and pressure. For example, *"I have to be responsible." "It's up to me." "If I don't do it, no one will."* When did this start in your story?

2. Consider what you would do with your time if you could do whatever you wanted. Often this reflects the design of who God made us to be. Discovering His design for us takes reflection and prayerful consideration of our stories, our wiring, and our desires. Think about what you dread doing in this season of life. (Doing things out of commitment or obedience is good, but we want to assess our motives and align our entire beings with the heart of God. Sometimes responsibility and duty become our idols rather than hearing from the One who made us.)

3. What would the people you love say they need most from you today? If you are not sure, take time to ask them. Take their input as information rather than a critique. You are offering a lifeline that will help you, them, and the relationship. You may not be able to meet the needs right away, but the feedback will give you a chance to hit a bull's-eye as you assess how you spend your time, money, and emotional resources.

4. Schedule a day once a month for quiet reflection. If you can manage a quarterly day or overnighter away for contemplative quiet space of internal reflection, this kind of slowing down will help you sustain the long haul of leadership.

5. Consider developing a hobby, and schedule time for it as you would for a business meeting. This is not a hobby for work (i.e., golfing with clients or coffee dates with volunteers). This is something you may have loved to do as a kid or have always wanted to try. (Jeff fly-fishes and finds that this activity fuels a deeper connection with God. Terra loves to create with her hands and enjoys time to paint, decorate her home, or create a homemade meal.) Slowing down can grow another side of you as you consider the good of life in the midst of all the hard.

6. Create with your hands. Try something like knitting or woodworking. Having something practical to do with our hands (outside of a digital device) reduces anxiety and releases pleasure hormones in the body.

7. Maybe it is time to see a good counselor to talk about all the concerns you are holding for the people you serve. A confidential setting without consequences can be the most powerful release of all the years of carrying other people's stuff. In fact, many leaders use therapists, spiritual directors, and executive coaches as part of their ongoing preventative care rather than waiting for burnout.

Chapter 10

ISOLATION

No One Really Knows Me

If we understand followership, we are well aware that
you can't separate how you live from how you lead.
—Joseph M. Stowell, *Redefining Leadership*

Most leaders never intend to be lonely. Yet there is something about the nature of leadership and influence that isolates a person. It becomes up to that leader to fight back in order to not be lost to the beast of leadership. "It is lonely at the top," the saying goes, "but you eat better."[1]

TERRA'S STORY

In my early twenties, I had the privilege of working full-time at a large suburban church outside greater Portland. As the first wholeness director, I helped oversee all the care ministries from addiction recovery and marriage mentoring to divorce care and grief support. While working, I was also finishing my master's in marriage and family therapy and participating in an internship at the county jail. (Like a good overachiever, I had to do it all at the same time.) A couple of days a week, I ventured to the county courthouse to get patted down by security guards and start my day with meth addicts, trafficked women, and spouses and children of batterers. Those drives from the neighboring county jail to my office at the church were times when God spoke deep truths into my soul that have greatly shaped what we do at Living Wholehearted today.

Though often divided by privilege, socioeconomics, religion, culture, and more, the stories in both locations revealed the weeds common to all our lives along with the hidden, stubborn root system of isolation. The symptoms looked different—one road led to illegal drug addiction, theft, and incarceration, and the other to an MBA, founding organizations, and late nights attempting to cope only to fall into pornography. A glass of wine and fresh lipstick could not cover over the loneliness and shame that were palpable in both groups. I found myself asking big questions about leadership, church systems, and the clever ways we hide, not with a wagging finger but to settle the unrest in my own soul. *Where are we doing this well?*

In both communities, people's stories were hemmed in by trauma, neglect, a lack of healthy models, and a sense that no one really saw them, knew them, or loved them. **When we don't have a relationship in which we experience the safety of being fully known and loved, our fear of rejection often outweighs our desire to be seen.** Beneath the surface were recurring themes of low self-worth and wondering whether God and others really liked them, considering all they were holding. Protective walls ran high, and maladaptive coping strategies were cleverly plotted to keep anyone from finding out. These walls and strategies, though not always obvious or intentional, are the result of the fall—when deciding to hide was our split-second reaction to recognizing our nakedness and feeling shame. Because of privilege and opportunity, one population washed away these feelings with performance and awe-inspiring agency in the world, while the other drowned in the systemic ripple effects of poverty and crime. The common link: loneliness.

Leaders seem to be the ones who silently suffer the most because of the weight of their impressive abilities and the number of people who look to them. The world has become increasingly connected, fixating on fame and quickly idealizing anyone with a turnaround story. As a result, we have designated one set of weeds as the pretty ones, even though their invasive nature destroys any form of life underground. These particular types of weeds have preyed on me most of my life, both in the literal sense as a novice gardener and in the figurative sense as a high-capacity leader.

DEFINING ISOLATION

I was a sophomore in high school when I first experienced the reality of leader loneliness. I had recently moved to the Northwest after spending my whole life in the desert of Arizona. I started over in a new town, new school, and new culture, but within a month of being on campus, I was nominated to homecoming court. As the new girl on a high school campus of nearly two thousand students, the loneliness I felt amid immediate popularity confused me. God was giving me favor through the varsity volleyball team and advanced courses, yet I confused His favor with what I truly needed: *real relationships*. No one *really* knew me. The packaged first-impression version of me was desperately trying to make a way in a new school after leaving the only home I knew.

Rather than processing my overwhelming grief, I turned to performing—a common theme in my younger years and for many leaders.

I did not like the way it felt to be unseen, so I spent time pursuing and seeing those in front of me. When I felt lonely, I looked for another lonely person in the room, and sometimes that person was the least likely suspect. God built me to listen to and see those who get missed in a crowd; whether popular or outcast, all are the same to me. This others-focused approach seems harmless and is even taught from the pulpit and in Sunday schools, yet it leaves a bitter aftertaste. Initially it offers feel-good moments, but it provides no lasting depth of relationship.

My coping strategy felt good to others, and I was quickly looked to as someone who made anyone feel at ease. For example, I remember intentionally sitting with kids who had special needs during lunch. Other leaders would join, like our school quarterback, Brock Huard (who went on to play in the NFL and become a sports analyst). These were really thoughtful things and were coming from a genuine place, but serving others without ever letting anyone into my inner world became a pattern that lasted long after high school. I was attempting to do good while ignoring my own feelings deep inside, putting my energy into serving those around me. This type of behavior is championed in the church and can lead to dysfunctional patterns. I benefited from a dangerous system we have created in both sacred and secular cultures. Beneath the layers of my good behavior, awards, accolades, and desire to give to others, I was seen as good to go. My heart was rarely pursued.

The longer I lived in the lane of leadership, fewer people considered my personal journey to be important. A common theme for many. Rarely was I asked how I was doing. **I did not know how to let others see me without performing, and I do not think they knew how to see me.** Permission is needed from both parties to move to deeper soil. God forbid that I should say I was lonely or needed more from anyone. It looked like I had it all, and admitting loneliness would have felt petty and selfish. I had friends galore, and everyone knew my name, yet at the end of the day, I would go home and write to God in my journals. Only He understood my longing for something deeper. The angst in my soul fueled an eating disorder I kept hidden for many years.

Assuming a leader's health and capacity works just fine when someone is healthy. Yet we would bet that high-functioning, impressive people are actually running from the voices they hear inside their heads and need trusted relationships to help ground them. We have a tendency to look at capacity and rush the time we should take to understand someone's character development and story. We have already discussed how greatly our stories affect who we are and how we function. Again and again while working with leaders, I have heard statements similar to my own: "Rarely was I asked how I was doing. *I did not know how to let others see me.*"

Leadership creates environments of isolation, so not traveling the road alone takes intentionality. Whether it's imposter syndrome, a lack of trust, insufficient modeling, comparison, or a need for heroes, it's hard to tell if leaders isolate themselves or if followers keep leaders isolated. One seasoned leader who saw the potential in my gifts, talents, and wiring invited me into a mentoring relationship, and I quickly accepted, humbled by her offer. Though her mentorship was vital to my early development, I have been haunted by a passing comment she made one day as we ate lunch together. I asked her a simple and innocent question about who was mentoring her or investing in her life as she was giving to all those around her. She sadly responded, "The higher you go in your leadership, you will find it's a lonely place. There is no one, and it's part of what you need to be prepared for." *Gulp.* The normalizing tone this executive leader used to declare her view was startling, to say the least. I recognized in this paradigm a glaring problem that needed to be fixed, but I later heard this idea repeated by other respected leaders.

> Loneliness is not unique to leaders, but how are their followers to learn what trusted relationships look like when leaders normalize and accept loneliness as the cost of the call?

In that moment I began to fear success and did everything in my power to prevent moving up the ladder. For a time, keeping relationships intact was more important than trusting God with the call on my life. I would have chosen to stay connected to my community rather than be a high-capacity leader. As God reminds me of that conversation, I see how my smoldering hope of changing that paradigm has turned into a blazing fire. Loneliness is not unique to leaders, but how are their followers to learn what trusted relationships look like when leaders normalize and accept loneliness as the cost of the call? As a female leader, I see an even greater cost, as women have an innate sense of competition that can feed this isolation. More driven women, particularly in church culture, are often dismissed by both men and other women. This has many complex reasons behind it, but we hope it is slowly shifting for the better, as I addressed in my first book, *Courageous: Being Daughters Rooted in Grace.*

In the end, I realized the advice this leader gave came from her pain. But God's design is not for leaders to be isolated and unprotected from themselves and the snare of others. Isolated leaders are vulnerable and cannot see themselves accurately. Wholehearted Leaders recognize their need for others.

IN THE BIBLE

Loneliness is a human struggle that started in the garden of Eden. In the Genesis account, even though God walked with Adam and provided everything he needed, He said just before creating Eve, "It is not good for the man to be alone" (2:18). If we are made in God's image, then we are made for relationship. Our triune God lives in perfect community as the Father, the Son, and the Holy Spirit. Before the fall in chapter 3, Eve and Adam experienced perfect companionship with God and each other. But Eve believed the lie of the serpent, who told her that God did not mean what He said and had ulterior motives. The twinge of doubt—*Does He really want what is best for me, or is He holding out?*—influenced their decision to eat from the tree God said was not good for them. Their discontent and the pull of doing things their own way led Adam and Eve toward choices that would affect every generation. Even in the garden, where being known and loved was complete, humanity was still tempted and tried to hide. Despite our selfish bent toward doing life on our own and staying hidden, God's heart to protect us is seen in the creation of relationships.

After Adam and Eve ate the fruit, they hid from God, who had been present with them and communicating in ways they could hear and respond to. God did not come after them to shame them. He did not ask "Where are you?" because He did not know. Rather, He was giving them dignity by allowing them to decide between staying hidden and coming out and being known, a choice they knew would be painful. Not knowing the full ramifications, for the first time they felt deep-seated guilt that convicted them of their mistrust of God.

Few emerging leaders are warned about the hidden costs of leading, including the common realities of isolation, distance, and loneliness. Jesus' disciples were so excited to lead. In Mark 10 we find James and John boldly asking Jesus, "Let one of us sit at your right and the other at your left in your glory." I imagine Jesus' facial expression being so kind and patient while His words held enormous weight. "You don't know what you are asking" (vv. 37–38).

So often we ask God to give us favor without knowing what we are actually asking. Our limited understanding gives us grandiose ideas about what we can handle or what we are entitled to for "His glory." Peter was certain he would always be faithful to Jesus, declaring after the Last Supper, "Even if all fall away on account of you, I never will…. Even if I have to die with you, I will never disown you." Scripture says, "All the other disciples said the same" (Matt. 26:33–35). *You mean Peter wasn't the only one who thought he would never struggle in his allegiance to his Savior and his call? I love the reality of the Word!* We know Peter later denied Jesus three times, as He predicted. Though Peter was cemented in his self-confidence, Jesus knew Peter's utter humanity was too fragile and would not withstand the pressures that lay ahead (see vv. 69–75).

(Terra) I took a spiritual inventory as a young leader, and it told me I was like Peter. Hmm … how should one take that? Half of me thought, *Wow, the entire church was built on Peter's passionate boldness and obedience.* The other half of me knew the stories of his finicky passion: one moment on fire and the next weeping bitterly as he fell prey to the Enemy's tactics. That reality check sobered me up as I prayerfully journaled, asking for a steadfast faith that would remain humble and rooted regardless of the tests of time. Passionate people make great movers and shakers. They are founders, entrepreneurs, pioneers, and creators. Passionate people can also find themselves lying in bed with the covers over their heads, saying they want to quit when the crowds change their tone. I would know. The test said I was like Peter. And years later, after shedding tears of self-pity, I can see why. *Pray for Jeff.*

> Do you have trusted people in place to remind you of who God is and who you are in Him?

The good news is that Jesus appeared to Peter after His death and miraculous resurrection (see John 21:15–19). Peter was one of the first to experience His grace, to experience the touch of His faithfulness regardless of the tendency of our faith to waver. You *will* struggle as a leader (you already have if you are seasoned). It is only a matter of time before you will wrestle against the pull of your flesh and fight battles for your influence. Do you have trusted people in place to remind you of who God is and who you are in Him?

THE LIE

As humans we are attracted to leadership, but this attraction makes us vulnerable to making and reinforcing misguided assumptions about how leaders should appear and what they should do for us. **We are prone to overidealizing status and imagining what it might be like in a leader's shoes—being compensated at higher levels, overseeing great teams, being heard, and seeing our vision come to life.** Many wonderful internal and external benefits come with leadership, but it also comes with a number of costs often not perceived by aspiring leaders, followers, and those in leadership positions for a while. For many, loneliness becomes so "normal" it isn't recognized any longer, similar to sitting in a heavily perfumed room and finding that the strength of the aroma becomes less noticeable the longer one remains in the room. What once was repulsive or tear-producing is now unnoticed and forgotten. Leaders become accustomed to loneliness and isolation, often missing the impact on their minds, bodies, souls, and relationships.

(Jeff) I was recently sitting with a few friends discussing the challenge it is for many of us guys to accurately perceive our feelings. Who cares what we might be feeling, and who has the time to reflect even if we're curious? We just plow forward. One of my friends, John, was trying to trace patterns of feelings about being a leader and how his role isolated him during his workday. He realized he didn't have any friends at work who weren't looking to please him because of his power and authority. He wondered, "How often am I actually feeling lonely (or other feelings) at work?" He found an app that let him record in one word how he felt at different moments throughout his day. After collecting his responses over a week and charting them, he realized that loneliness was a pattern, and it felt good to recognize his feelings and name them.

The reality is that when we take positions of leadership in any organization, the relational dynamics change for all the players. Fellow leaders, past coworkers, spouses, families, friends, churches, and teams are all impacted, and often the change doesn't sit well with everyone it touches. The temptation to isolate ourselves in response can be resisted if we allow friends to journey with us as we gain greater influence.

If you are an emerging leader, it would benefit you to reflect on the ways that holding a leadership role you aspire to could create emotional and physical distance in valued relationships. For example, if you and a colleague whom you consider a friend are working at similar levels within a company, you likely enjoy daily time when you interact and share stories and experiences related to your day-to-day tasks and responsibilities. Advancing in the company is something you both may aspire to for many of the reasons we've mentioned.

Consider the following scenario: One day, after being recognized for your strong performance and the way others on the team lean on you, your boss shares with you that there will be an opening in the department and she wants you to consider stepping into the management role. In this scenario, your colleague/friend would be reporting to you, and you would be responsible for evaluating him. His live-lihood is suddenly tied to decisions you make. At this news, your colleague/friend may be authentically happy for you and encourage you to take the position. However, the reality is you will automati-cally introduce a new and potentially challenging dynamic into the relationship you presently enjoy. His comfort in talking candidly about life and humorous things is likely to change and would need to change to maintain a level of professionalism and health for both of you, the team, and the organization. A new level of emotional and physical distance would occur and, depending on how you are wired, would affect you in different ways.

On the flip side, imagine if you maintained the relationship the way it had been before you assumed the leadership role. This could be draining for you in a different way and affect the credibility you seek to gain and sustain in your efforts to lead. Are the pay increase, the new title, and the office worth it? Is this what God is asking of you? It may be, but it would be wise to consider the costs in light of *who you are* and *what you need* to thrive.

You face a big decision as you weigh the lure of a leadership role against the challenge of changing the type of relationship you have with your colleague/friend. Seeking out other voices in your life is vital. You will want to connect with mentors who have a practical perspective that will help you navigate these relational shifts well. Unpack fears and weigh the pros and cons of your current versus your potential role. As you verbally process with another human being, you're likely to gain the clarity you seek.

The wisdom and insights provided by the Core Values Index can also help us process healthier ways to not isolate or live out of conflict. Using the job-opening example, a Merchant sees the world in terms of people and relationships. A Banker generally wants and (depending on the importance of the matter) needs more time than most to read and analyze things that are being presented. Details about a change in role and work relationships would take awhile to collect and process. Though a Merchant needs to verbally process to make sense of his inner life, a Banker works from the inside out and needs someone to wait patiently for her to make conclusions from facts and evidence about what she needs, the system needs, and her colleague needs.

For an Innovator, the proposed changes might be exciting. The moment the boss talks to him about the coming vacancy, he thinks he could be considered for a promotion. Innovators hold complexity and are thinking on many levels, so he likely considers several other factors simultaneously, including how the position might affect his relational dynamics with his colleague/friend. And last, a Builder might be the most inclined to seize an opportunity like this without adequately reflecting on the relational implications. A Builder's core value of power is linked both to a desire to use her personal energy to make a positive difference and to her faith, which is an innate sense of knowing what to do when action is needed. Many leaders at the top of their organizations have a high Builder score.

SHRINKING THIS GAP

For many like my friend John, isolation is a real feeling faced on a fairly regular basis. John decided to do something to get his needs for authentic relationship and friendship met in a healthy way at his workplace. He joined an on-campus Bible study that met either before work or on break. He also meets regularly with a leadership coach with whom he can be candid about the people issues he is sorting out while continuing to face the growth edges he and his coach identify together.

Another way to combat seclusion is to seek out professional groups and online forums for leaders at all levels to meet, discuss, and journey together. However, don't discount the deeper connections of friendship, where a person will see you not just for your titles, big-time projects, or influence. **A large part of the solution for leaders is to find healthy rhythms of rest and rituals they keep outside work with people who bring them life.** No matter how we're wired, we all need rest and space to rejuvenate with people we trust and know will generously give to us, not judge us.

THE ROLE OF COMMUNITY

One of the biggest blessings in our own lives has been our community group. For years these special couples and families have helped us combat the isolation and loneliness of leadership. For a married couple whose lives are intertwined from work to play, we need extra layers of protection. As we teach and help others, we are accountable for staying aware and putting habits in place to push against the natural pulls of leadership.

Our community group experience through the years has been powerful and humbling, challenging us in tough times to move toward others rather than pull away. Several years ago, we moved to a rural area about twenty-five minutes from our home church. It would have been easy for us to isolate ourselves in the woods, but we recognized our need for connection. We decided to invite other couples and families in our local community whom we casually met in the public schools, at coffee shops, on the field, and at the grocery store. Though a number of the couples did not initially have a vision for deeper community, we knew it was essential and willingly invested the time, energy, and vulnerability to create the invitation and build meaningful history. Time and consistency build trust.

We began by inviting couples we already saw in our day-to-day lives and whom we felt a nudge from the Holy Spirit to move toward. Though we did not all go to the same church, we all had a common vision of living with intentionality as we raised our kids. Eight other couples said yes to our invitation. We began meeting twice a month during the school year to grow in our faith and friendship and to start something else we had been dreaming about: a group called Courageous Girls—now a global movement we founded to help moms (and dads) and daughters at every stage of their developing years.[2]

We're now many years in, and these friends have become like air to us. We share a commitment to becoming more like Jesus in our marriages, families, and neighborhoods. From the outset, having people from different churches added depth, diversity, and appreciation for the greater body of Christ. Not everyone in our group is a high-capacity leader or has a calling as broad as ours, but our love and care for one another is rich and marked by the daily practice of 1 Corinthians 13: "Love … always protects, always trusts, always hopes, always perseveres" (vv. 6–7). That's it. God chose these friends for us and us for them, and together we are choosing to love the community He gave us and to receive love in return.

We recommend letting go of human systems that require keeping up appearances and instead developing a rhythm that moves you toward transformation by God. This happens when we lower our barriers and expectations of *how* relationships, community, or church is supposed to look and instead move toward commitment, consistency, and honesty with others. The brokenness of humanity can certainly disappoint. The discipline of staying rooted in a community comes from releasing our ideals and focusing on the practice of being known and knowing others. Dietrich Bonhoeffer said it this way: "The person who loves their dream of community will destroy community, but the person who loves those around them will create community."[3]

(Terra) In my earlier married years, I spent time getting my nails done and had fake ones. I think it had to do with rediscovering my femininity after years of being a tomboy. The manicure would grow out every couple of weeks, leaving chipped paint and exposed cuticle beds. Looking back, those nails taught me a life lesson: It was easy to impress people with my beautiful nails when I kept them at a distance, waving my hand from a stage or across the room. However, the moment I let people see my hands up close, the ugly parts of those nails were visible.

The temptation for leaders is to keep everyone at a distance, but we all need at least a few people whom we let see our ugly exposed cuticle beds. When we realize the freedom in letting go of expectations and welcoming others in, we end up knowing, on a *ginōskō* gut level, that we are loved because of who we are, not because of what we do. *Ginōskō* is the Greek word for "know" in the New Testament. It's the kind of knowing that can only come from experience, rather than information.[4] This kind of knowing increases our chances of sustaining the long and enduring race of leadership without losing ourselves in the journey. **Many leaders, though well liked and loved by many, are without a "home" where they actually are known by and know others on a deep level.** If you have this, be grateful. If you don't, start praying for the "who." You may need to initiate, but watch and see what God does with your obedience.

Many in the younger generation have swung the pendulum away from isolation toward the opposite extreme. In their hunger for authenticity, they often lack discernment regarding with whom and how much to share. One of the results of trauma is that our trust meters are broken. We can become extremely guarded, trusting no one, or we can become inappropriately exposing, trusting everyone. With the rise of the digital age, the lack of models, the starvation for community, and the fast pace of stardom, what we publicly expose of our stories must be carefully considered. There is a level of transparency that followers desire and yet is not appropriate for the masses. Actually, being deeply known by a few allows us to be more authentic and trusted by many.

This last year, as we wrote this book and faced some of the hardest struggles in our marriage (stories for another book), I recall my dearest friend saying, "I am worried about you, Terra." I was annoyed at first (*I am fine*), then became defensive (*I got this*). Finally, I heard the Holy Spirit's gentle whisper, *Let her in. This is why she is in your life.* Building trusted relationships with our community group took a couple of years of great courage, patience, forgiveness, and help as we continued to turn toward one another. It's not ideal, perfect, or easy all the time, but we are all choosing to lay down our masks and be known. That kind of risk and vulnerability is holy ground, especially when one has experienced a breach of trust and carries scars from previous relationships. As Harville Hendrix said, "We are born in relationship, we are wounded in relationship, and we can be healed in relationship."[5]

THE CALL

Leadership can be attractive for many reasons: more money, more perks, more freedom, and more power. It's easy not only to crave what we think leaders have but also to start believing we have to act and look the part to get there. Certainly, the media and celebrity leaders reinforce this through music, movies, magazines, news, TED talks, and glamorized award shows. Even the church glorifies the lives of people with significant talent.

If we're not careful, it doesn't take long to start believing our own press (good or bad). We start thinking, as James and John did after hanging with Jesus for a while, that we deserve more. Misplaced faith and hope, unrealistic expectations of self and others, entitlement, and believing the voices around us all add up. We're not advocating for emerging leaders not to have faith or dream *big*. In fact, we believe those dreams are often knit into the DNA of a person, placed with great intention and purpose by the Creator. We are simply advocating for bringing forth dreams and passions under the protection and within the confines of trusted and safe relationships with God and others.

We're all hardwired with a need to be known by and to know others, and leaders are no exception. **Time and consistency build trust.** God knows we need others for our journey through the highs and lows of life and the unique stresses of leadership. It's not good for anyone to be alone. Who are your people?

Key Markers of Isolation

• You notice a disconnect between what you say and what you actually think and feel.

• You are limited by the role you play in people's lives. If someone were to tell you the truth, it would alter the nature of your relationship.

• You feel lonely under the weight of what you carry but turn to no one.

• You don't have a 3 a.m. friend—someone you can call with any need or emergency, even at 3 a.m.

• You question who your friends are and who is connected to you only because of work.

Antidotes

1. Name one to three people you will ask to meet with weekly for one year. Practice doing a check-in. If this is completely new to you, start by sharing from your week: (a) What was your high? (b) What was your low? (c) What did you learn about God, yourself, or others?

2. In order to get below the surface, try this exercise: Draw a simple tree. Name the current fruits of your life. Are they fruits of the Spirit, or are you seeing anger, resentment, competitiveness, or arrogance? Then move to the roots and name the hidden parts of your life. Things you think, feel, or do when no one is looking. What are you seeing? Ask God to help you see what He's seeing in you. Does anyone else in your life know this part of you?

3. Prayerfully ask God to search you and show you what vows you have made to never let anyone hurt you again. Where did those vows originate in your story?

4. Do you sabotage people trying to know you beyond your role as a leader? If you do, consider asking one to three trusted friends to help you understand more of how they see this tendency and their thoughts on why you might be doing this.

5. Consider creating a covenant with a couple of friends. These need to be outside your marriage, if you are married. Write up what you will do for each other and how you will turn toward one another when one of you is believing your own press (positive or negative) or when the life of leadership is too heavy to carry alone. Develop a rhythm of reevaluating this contract regularly, and don't forget to celebrate together as this covenant friendship endures!

Chapter 11

SURVIVAL

Needs Are a Sign of Weakness

*Courage is not something that you already
have that makes you brave when the tough
times start. Courage is what you earn when
you've been through the tough times and you
discover they aren't so tough after all.*
—Malcolm Gladwell, *David and Goliath*

Trauma teaches us that our needs do not matter. Whether it's an
out-of-control experience like an earthquake or a violent outburst
from an angry alcoholic father, survival supersedes needs. Children
who learn to ignore their own emotional and psychological needs in
order to keep their alcoholic parent "happy" or who receive focused
attention from their successful parents only when they perform well
can develop into leaders who learn to ignore their own needs and, in
turn, the needs of those they lead. The higher we go in leadership,
the more vulnerable we become to having our outer needs met but
our inner needs ignored.

DEFINING NEEDS

Maslow's hierarchy of needs, a psychological theory originally articulated in the early 1940s,[1] suggests that before one can discover higher levels of functioning, such as cognitive needs or self-actualization, basic physiological, safety, and belonging needs must be met. There are ways for children—who didn't have some of their basic needs met—to achieve what might *look like* higher levels of functioning, but the basic emotional needs of every human being still need to be addressed.

> Every human has the God-given need to matter to someone, whether we sit behind bars, the pulpit, or the CEO desk.

In a room of world changers from all over, executive leaders from Prison Fellowship shared how they moved from the prison system to new lives of leadership. (Terra) I was struck by Sarah. Close to sixty years lining her face, she grinned from ear to ear as she spoke of the women she was privileged to walk with in the prison systems. As a young girl who was trapped in a life of sex trafficking, drugs, and crime, she knew only the piles of shame that suffocated her while living in and out of the prison system. Someone from the audience asked what she had not received in her home as a young child that may have contributed to the years she spent in prison. The questioner was trying to uncover how kids caught in the Department of Human

Services (DHS) system might have a fighting chance for a different outcome. Sarah confidently answered, "If you don't matter to your parents, you feel like you don't matter." She went on to explain that it was the Prison Fellowship ladies who came in week after week "who loved me like I mattered." She continued, "Because they saw me, met my basic human needs to be seen and loved, I began to heal and years later got to where I am today."[2] Every human has the God-given need to matter to someone, whether we sit behind bars, the pulpit, or the CEO desk.

THE LIE

Every child is created with innate needs: to be seen, loved, valued as significant, and safe. Without these essential ingredients in our childhood—whether our parents could not provide them because of their own trauma or they ignored them to prioritize comfort, activities, and success—kids suffer and are stunted. Learning to identify our needs, ask for help, receive comfort for those needs, and then offer that same comfort to others who have needs is foundational to becoming a healthier, whole person.[3] Yet something changes as we grow older and start to fend for ourselves. Society has created and nurtured an ideology that says the more mature you are, the less you need. This could not be further from the truth. In actuality, the more you mature, the more you recognize your needs and are able to meet them in a thirst-quenching way.

God has provided legitimate ways for meeting the legitimate needs He created. However, many times we dismiss legitimate needs, mistaking them for wants or calling them weaknesses. This leads to a life of seeking to meet legitimate needs in illegitimate ways—stress release through drinking, intimacy through pornography, significance through workaholism, or justice through anger.

We have heard countless Christian leaders quote the apostle Paul in Philippians 3:13–15: "Brothers and sisters, I do not consider myself yet to have taken hold of it. But one thing I do: Forgetting what is behind and straining toward what is ahead, I press on toward the goal to win the prize for which God has called me heavenward in Christ Jesus. All of us, then, who are mature should take such a view of things. And if on some point you think differently, that too God will make clear to you." But Paul did not mean we should honor the lack of awareness that so many leaders take as maturity. He was not saying we should push past our needs, running a race without the basics of water, food, injury prevention, and crowd control (to stretch the analogy). Paul processed his past in many other passages, and if we read between the lines of Scripture, it's clear that Paul *did* the work (maybe not in a counseling office or with a leadership coach) of processing his past, present, and future through the lens of his new identity in Christ.

STORIES OF UNMET NEEDS

(Terra) One day in my office, Nate, a highly influential Christian leader, shared how every success in his early life had been stolen by his mother's need to share that success with all their family and friends. His success (or lack of success) quickly became about her. His healthy need was to be acknowledged and to have his contributions seen and celebrated. Instead, his unmet need left him unconsciously craving to be the star in every room he entered. In pursuing a life of stellar performance, he still failed to see his insatiable need for recognition.

Nate excelled in everything he did, yet he could not express emotion or a need for love, comfort, and care. He saw his children as a reflection of himself (repeating what his mom did to him). In unpacking his sexual intimacy struggles, his wife, Sandy, shared that she could not compliment him enough. She found that his lack of rest, intense need for greatness, and impenetrable exterior would not allow anyone in the home to be human. His sexual desire for his wife was the only way he found solace in his treadmill of a life. Nate was actually modeling how to stuff, ignore, and hide his humanity. (In some circles, we might even call this emotional neglect.)

When I asked Nate what his family did together, he looked at me with a blank stare and said, "We don't. We are in our own rooms, on our devices, or so busy we rarely see each other." Their dinner table conversation consisted of a report of activities and stories about others in the community. This leader gave his life for his family, church, and employees. When I followed up with "What do you need in your marriage?" he responded, "I don't have needs. Those are a sign of weakness." I looked at Sandy and asked, "What is it like for you to hear him say that?" She replied with little to no emotion, "It sounds about right. That means my children cannot have needs. I surely cannot have needs. We are the family that helps others with *their* needs."

In the recent past, it was rare in America to hear people publicly expressing their needs. Most businesses and organizations honored the chain of command, where executives at the top spoke to one another and only a few below them on the org chart. The supervisor and direct-report hierarchy continued down from the top. It was rare for leaders to consider emotional needs as anything but irrational and unnecessary. Whether in the home around siblings, in a classroom setting, or in a conference room, people just didn't ask for help in front of others. Now the pendulum has swung so far the other direction that children, youth, and young adults think that any uncomfortable urge is a "need" and that someone else is responsible for satisfying it ASAP. In a way, we have developed a bottom-up approach to our way of being, allowing our emotions to dictate how we respond to our needs. Even more challenging is the reality that younger generations entering the workforce have lived most of their lives getting anything they want—information, food, and entertainment—in an instant. As the largest generation in the history of the world, millennials and their highly addictive desires are dictating the consumer market and will for the next several decades.

This ties back to the inherited baggage that millennials are carrying even though most aren't aware of it, let alone where it came from. Many, though not all, millennials live in a state of ambivalence. *Why can't I get ahead in my job? Why do I struggle to have actual friendships outside my online connections? Why do I get angry so fast? Why can't I overcome my anxiety and depression? Why do I feel so lonely?* For any generation, the answer lies in what we experienced when we were learning our first lessons at home from our primary caregivers, dad and mom.

FAMILY INFLUENCE

In their insightful book *How We Love*, Milan and Kay Yerkovich nail the importance and impact of our families of origin. A key point of the book is how our families affect our ability to thrive relationally (they hone in on the marriage relationship). This can be traced all the way back to whether we received enough comfort from our parents after experiences of emotional distress. Comfort has three components: touch, listening, and relief from whatever has hurt us.[4] If we experienced comfort often enough from childhood through youth, we likely developed a healthy attachment to our folks, which provided us with a road map for developing other healthy attachments. If we didn't receive comfort regularly enough in those critical years, we likely did not attach in a healthy way to our parents, and the pattern continues in our efforts to relate to others throughout our lives. Feelings and needs matter more than most ever imagine. There's actually good reason for that famous question we all expect to hear from mental health providers: "So, tell me about your childhood."

Our first relational lessons in our families of origin dramatically impact how we do life and relationships thereafter. The sad reality is that this truth is regularly dismissed, made light of, or even weaponized in our society and in the church today. You may know someone who has made a mantra of saying "Nothing bothers me" or "Suck it up" or "Don't be so sensitive!" Phrases like these are just another maladaptive coping strategy that people employ to avoid feeling emotions that likely need to be felt, understood, and dealt with in a healthy way so they don't creep up again and again! By using a command like "Don't be so sensitive!" to stop someone else from feeling, the person trying to avoid emotion is likely perpetrating the same abuse that he or she experienced earlier in life. A translation of "Don't be so sensitive!" might actually be something like "Will you quit with all this need to share what you're feeling about everything! It makes me *really* uncomfortable. I've spent the better part of my life trying not to feel anything because it doesn't feel good when I do!" **By avoiding deep relationships out of a need for self-protection, people will stay stuck in the damaging patterns they learned in their primary relationships.**

To heal and develop new neuropathways requires a safe environment and a trusted person to relate to over long periods of time. One of the systems in our brains that has fascinated researchers for the last few decades are mirror neurons, which help us mimic the behavior of those around us. Curt Thompson said it this way:

> If I see someone pick up a cup to drink from it, my mirror neurons will fire, preparing the 'mirrored' neurons responsible for picking up and drinking from a cup to fire.
>
> This has important implications for actions such as empathy. Empathy can be described as an action rather than merely a feeling alone because we *demonstrate* empathy through nonverbal and verbal cues or actions that project the *intent* of connecting with another's state of mind.... Children learn how to be empathic with others by seeing it demonstrated toward them.[5]

The good news is that our brains are not permanently fixed and can change as we experience new ways of thinking and relating to one another.

(Jeff) *Because we are all hardwired as human beings with a strong desire to be known and to know others*, I try to remember this when

I'm sitting in the office of a type-A leader who has a history of making himself or herself look big by making others look small. Whether a gas station attendant or a CEO, we are all the same at the core. There's nothing wrong with earning credentials, holding a high-level position, or having wealth, but it can insulate people from their real need to be known and to know others … their need for authentic relationships. So how can leaders meet their own need to be known and to know others while they manage the onslaught of tasks, requests, and five-alarm fires they have to put out on a daily basis? The answer is easier *and* harder than you might think!

> Our first relational lessons in our families of origin dramatically impact how we do life and relationships thereafter.

First things first: we have to recognize and name our own feelings, which cue us to our needs. Sometimes the body cues us before the mind does. Once we identify healthy ways to comfort those feelings, we can advocate for our needs instead of ignoring them or expecting someone else to meet them. This requires regular rhythms of slowing down and reflecting. Healthy routines of self-care (exercise, sleep, healthy eating, reading and reflecting on Scripture, prayer, and shared activity with family or a few key friends) are essential. Equally important is regular engagement with someone you consider a mentor and with someone you are mentoring. In these relationships, you should be yourself and share the load of what you're holding. These relationships help us identify our needs when we are overwhelmed or dismissive of our own humanity.

IN THE BIBLE

(Terra) In many Christian environments, needs get confused with sin. **A God-given need is always at the root of a sinful behavior or maladaptive coping strategy. But not every response to a God-given need is a sinful behavior.** The challenge is in understanding the difference and how to respond with grace. For example, I may need to verbally process some frustrations. I understand that God made me this way. I can admit my need to verbally process, but it would be sinful to go and gossip to several people to release my tensions and anxiety. If I don't tune in early enough when this need arises, my body starts to tell me: my gut starts to ache and my chest feels heavy. A healthy way to meet this need would be to start by journaling to God. If that is not enough, another way to meet this need is to go to my husband or my covenant friends to ask whether they can listen to me process this frustration. I am not sinning as I fling my hands in the air and passionately spit out my words. I am releasing, making sense of things, and finding comfort in appropriate places. The sin would be if I were to run to another man for emotional comfort, blast my unfiltered opinions about another person on social media, or stuff it all in until my body takes over and I start yelling at my children for no reason. The sinning is not in the need. The sinning is in ignoring the need and not taking it to the right places.

Taking our needs to the right places is a skill we learn early in life from our parents as we observe how attuned (or not) they were to our basic human needs. Leaders who appear stronger as they face the challenges of the day, not needing anyone else's help, likely grew up in chaotic homes with parents who were absent, overachievers, or avoiders. Ironically, followers like these seemingly confident leaders. With an innate need for a confident protector to lead us away from pain, we often do not realize our way must be *through* the pain, not around it. From a biblical worldview, being stronger means we acknowledge our needs and our inability to meet them on our own, lest we live lives of white-knuckling our way through the grime. First Peter 5:8 warns that we recognize our vulnerabilities lest we become prey: "Be alert and of sober mind. Your enemy the devil prowls around like a roaring lion looking for someone to devour."

The human desire to follow leaders who look and act a certain way and deliver in a particular and often unrealistic manner is part of the problem. As we discussed in chapter 4, ancient Israelites were enthralled with strong leaders, and they wanted someone of their choosing (we're not so different today). They longed to be like other nations that had a king. They had Yahweh (God) Himself as their perfect leader, but since He is spirit—not flesh and bone—they preferred a man for the job. Yahweh gave them what they wished for, as He so often does with His people, and Saul was appointed king.

Saul looked the part—tall, confident, strong, and handsome. The people's plan worked for a while until Saul began to rely on himself instead of staying submitted to Yahweh's guidance and commands as the true Commander in Chief. If only King Saul had stayed connected to his community and the vulnerabilities of his humanity. After the anointing and mantle of authority had been removed from

Saul by God Himself, his unlikely successor, David, was chosen. No
one from Jesse's family—and not even God's prophet (who was the
selection committee)—was thinking this shepherd boy was the right
man for the job. A leader's appearance or pedigree is often not what
we expect (see 1 Sam. 8–16).

God chose a different kind of leader. One who was writing songs
in the pastures, crying out to his God for help. David was a leader
who knew his needs and kept them in perspective—though he forgot
years later (a reminder to all of us). As David was being hunted by
Saul, he wrote Psalm 55:

> Listen to my prayer, O God,
>> do not ignore my plea;
>> hear me and answer me.
> My thoughts trouble me and I am distraught....
>
> My heart is in anguish within me;
>> the terrors of death have fallen on me.
> Fear and trembling have beset me;
>> horror has overwhelmed me....
>
> Cast your cares on the LORD
>> and he will sustain you;
> he will never let
>> the righteous be shaken....
>
> But as for me, I trust in you.
>> (vv. 1–2, 4–5, 22–23)

Saul believed his own press and felt threatened by David. Instead of recognizing his insecurity and jealousy, he took it on himself to meet his own need in a very unhealthy way—attempting to kill David. We later learn that David fell victim to the same trap for a time when he too began to believe his own press (see 1 Sam. 18–19; 2 Sam. 11). A Wholehearted Leader is not devoid of needs. **A Wholehearted Leader acknowledges needs and humbly submits to meeting them in healthy, God-designed ways.**

THE GOOD SHEPHERD

God describes us—His creation of both male and female, who creatively bear His likeness—as sheep. And from what we know from the abundant shepherd and sheep metaphors in the Bible, God loves sheep too. The interesting thing about sheep is that they are ridiculously unintelligent and can be incredibly stubborn, to their own demise. A flock of sheep will huddle together and literally starve to death rather than cross the smallest stream to get to a lush pasture that's close enough to see and smell. Shepherds have to intervene by grabbing the lead sheep by the ears and dragging it across the water boundary to the food source. Once the sheep see the lead sheep across and eating, the whole flock jumps the water as if it were nothing. We're like these sheep.

God, in His sovereignty, created us with the need to be led, protected, provided for, and loved as a good shepherd does for his sheep. God referred to Himself as the shepherd of His people, and He called the leaders of His followers shepherds (see Ezek. 34:11; Jer. 23:1). In the well-known Twenty-Third Psalm, the Lord, our

Shepherd, provided for David so he would not want for anything. He made David lie down when he needed rest, providing green pastures with quiet waters for his restoration. The Good Shepherd guided David so he could walk in righteous ways (ways that reflect a right relationship with God). God's presence resulted in comfort and security for David. He could walk through the valley of the shadow of death and fear no evil (see vv. 1–4).

In the New Testament, Jesus told the parable of the lost sheep: the shepherd leaves the ninety-nine he's counted to find the one that has strayed (see Luke 15:3–7). In John 10 Jesus described Himself as "the good shepherd [who] lays down his life for the sheep" (v. 11). Although God created us with a nature like sheep (that's humbling), He has called and raised up other shepherds of our own kind to follow His lead and shepherd the flock in His ways. Wherever you may be leading, you are a shepherd leading sheep.

Nothing's changed since the first leaders were called and emerged on the landscape to inspire, serve, govern, and rule. Good shepherds lead by being present, aware, and attentive to the needs of their flock. They do this best when they have experienced what it's like to get their own needs met. At His core, God, the Good Shepherd, is leading out of love for His sheep. Sometimes it feels like we're being dragged by the ears across boundaries we've built, when in fact they are nothing to Him. He knows that if we won't move, we'll starve to death in our anxiety, fear, stubbornness, or lack of vision. At times He intervenes but only because He loves us. We also know that the Good Shepherd stands at the doors of our lives and knocks, wanting us to invite Him in and trust Him to be our leader (see Rev. 3:20). **Every earthly shepherd needs the Good Shepherd. And every sheep needs a shepherd who knows the ways of the Good Shepherd.**

Despite the many beautiful Good Shepherd and sheep metaphors we find throughout the Old and New Testaments, we also see stern warnings for shepherds, especially in spiritual leadership, who choose to serve themselves instead of their flocks. Trying to meet their needs in unhealthy ways—ways outside God's design—puts their sheep in harm's way. Jeremiah the prophet wrote,

> "Woe to the shepherds who are destroying and scattering the sheep of my pasture!" declares the LORD. Therefore this is what the LORD, the God of Israel, says to the shepherds who tend my people: "Because you have scattered my flock and driven them away and have not bestowed care on them, I will bestow punishment on you for the evil you have done," declares the LORD. (Jer. 23:1–2)

Jeremiah went on to promise that God Himself would gather His flock and place other shepherds over them who would care for their needs and protect them (see vv. 3–4).

Given God's clear message that He is the shepherd and we are His sheep, why do we resist being led? Why do we believe we know better than God how to meet our needs? Even worse, why do we downplay our needs because we think they make us look weak? We cannot give away what we have not yet received. Many shepherds (leaders) are not willing to submit to the same process they expect their sheep to go through. One reason is that because so many leaders have unresolved trauma leaking into their lives and leadership, they are just trying to survive, coping as they did in their earlier years. They are still proving themselves rather than accepting what has already been given to them: the DNA of our God. God places a high priority on caring for His sheep well through good shepherding. Our dependence on the Good Shepherd should sober all leaders.

How we lead matters. How we lead as Christians really matters! God doesn't expect non-Christians to submit to His standards. They are lost and blind. But He certainly expects Christian shepherds to be accountable to His ways of leading. God holds the leaders who identify as His children—those who have chosen to surrender their lives to Christ—to a higher standard. Jesus' strongest rebukes were to the religious leaders and the shepherds of Israel. This is not about being perfect leaders; this is about being humble leaders who understand our own vulnerability as humans. We are to steward the knowledge, gifts, and resources He makes available to us and use them to serve by His power, in His name.

SHRINKING THIS GAP

We work with many men and women who, as good shepherds following the lead Shepherd, really want to lead well. They are actually shrinking their gaps while each day influencing their churches, parachurch organizations, communities, families, and businesses in small and big ways. They have our support, and we say, "Stay the course!"

Regardless of their foundation, leaders have unique responsibilities and are held to higher standards of accountability. The
consequence of leaders not living and leading with integrity is a wide
wake of damage. These realities and biblical warnings should give
us pause as we consider leadership aspirations and the importance
of shrinking the integrity gaps in our own lives. The weight of these
truths should not bind us in fear but rather lead us to a greater passion for growth and wholeness. A life of leadership is not meant to
be a burdensome "have to" but a "get to" as we lead according to His
power within us (see Eph. 3:16–21).

> Modeling the integration of mind, body,
> heart, and soul is a powerful kind of
> leadership.

**Wholehearted Leaders understand there is no need to prove
themselves.** They know they are adored and chosen by God, and they
consider every day to be a gift. Their identity as sons and daughters is
secure. Each opportunity or challenging circumstance is a chance to
grow closer to Him and be helped by Him. Nothing is owed to them
or seen as a result of their own hand. Like David, who was chosen
to lead when a shepherd boy, very few of us are chosen because of
anything other than God's grace.

The best leaders we've known, whether parents, pastors, church
elders, middle management, or CEOs, are those who follow the
wisdom found in John 15. Read these words in reference to being a

Wholehearted Leader, one *you* would want to follow. "I am the vine; you are the branches.... Apart from me you can do nothing" (v. 5). Let us aspire to stay connected to the greatest leader of all time, Jesus. His thoughts and ways are attractive, and we need to allow ourselves to be transformed into His likeness as we stand in awe of His glory and holiness. We must step humbly, recognizing that we cannot do this alone, and then submit to others who are experienced, wise, and trustworthy. When we fall short, we can pause and ask ourselves what need we're trying to get recognized. A pattern of mistakes may be a clue to a childhood wound—an unmet need that requires grace, time, and tender attention.

Modeling the integration of mind, body, heart, and soul is a powerful kind of leadership. Integration is key to living and leading with greater integrity. This requires connecting to the past and its impact on the present, discerning between wants and needs, and learning to be fully known in a safe environment. If this hard work is done, it can literally transform our neuropathways. Because wholehearted leadership requires vulnerability on the part of leaders—and because our culture promotes the opposite—safe, confidential environments are scarce! Discerning our deepest needs from our wants helps us focus our energy on what really matters. Jesus encouraged us to come to Him with the faith of a little child (see Matt. 18:2–3). As we become more attuned to our childlike needs, leaning into the grace of Christ, who suffered and died for us, we practically shrink our gaps and model to others that it's okay to do the same. We can rest in the assurance that our needs will be met.

Key Markers of Survival

- You find yourself ignoring your own needs. You feel selfish and weak, as if focusing on yourself would be gluttony.
- You recognize a need, but instead of acknowledging it, you dismiss it, minimize it, or overspiritualize it.
- You tough it out with self-talk like "Suck it up."
- You lack boundaries and do not know your limits. You might find yourself with unexplained physical ailments.
- You feel numb and unaffected by the pain of your own story or others'. You stay logical and rarely enter into your emotions or the emotions of others.

Antidotes

1. Identify five needs you have. Do not judge them. Do not analyze them as wants or desires or research Greek or Hebrew words related to *needs*. Prayerfully consider what you wanted and needed most as a child. What do you want and need more of today?

2. Take these needs to your safe relationships, and begin to unpack how you can meet those needs in a healthy way.

3. Are you focusing on climbing the capacity ladder or the character ladder? Check out this resource for more information: *The Ascent of a Leader* by Bill Thrall, Bruce McNicol, and Ken McElrath. Follow it by reading *The Cure* by Thrall, McNicol, and John Lynch.

4. Practice the exercise below for uncovering your emotions.[6] Remember that it can take years to discover how to do this if you were not taught how in your home or were shamed when expressing needs. Have grace for the process, recognizing that this is not an easy skill.

   • Identify what you are feeling (loneliness, fear, shame, inadequacy, anger).

   • Where is it located in your body (face, back, stomach, chest)?

   • What do you need to feel peace or comfort (a journaling session, a good cry, a workout, a hug)?

   • Advocate for that need.

   • Trust God and another person to help you meet your need in a healthy way. What truth or principle in God's Word do you need to remember in order to stay rooted?[6]

Chapter 12

HIDING

Confession Costs Too Much

You can't become a decent horseman until you fall off and get up again a good number of times. There's life in a nutshell.
—Bear Grylls, *Mud, Sweat, and Tears*

The fool tries to adjust the truth so he does not have to adjust to it.
—Henry Cloud, *Necessary Endings*

Purity of intention is really a reflection of the heart.…
The heart of a person with integrity always wants to do what's right, once he or she is sure what "right" is.
—John Wooden, *Coach Wooden's Pyramid of Success*

Those of us in leadership roles for a few years or more have probably done our fair share of confronting and have maybe heard our fair share of confessions. We wish we saw more voluntary and authentic confessions from the wise. Our triune God designed us, His image bearers, for relationships. To stay healthy we need to confess to God and to one another, and so experience the cathartic results. When we confess to God, we are forgiven, like releasing a helium balloon into the air. However, when we confess to one another, we are actually healed.

One of our core convictions is that God wants *all* of who we are: mind, body, heart, soul, actions, and relationships. The only way this can happen is when we fall, we come out of hiding and, baring every crevice of our souls, allow God and others to enter into our failures. How a person responds when confronted or after confession says a lot about the status of his or her heart. In his book *Necessary Endings*, Cloud reminded us, "You cannot deal with everyone in the same way."[1] The Bible, and many other experts who study human behavior, describe three kinds of people and their responses to failure and correction. We have taken the concept of these three categories and applied additional trauma research and our own professional experiences, and we use the analogy of a traffic signal. Traffic lights give drivers clear direction on the road, making it possible to have more confidence and peace when driving. A green light says "go" with ease. A yellow light means "yield," and we move forward with caution. A red light means "stop."

First, green-light people recognize their failures and the ways they've harmed others and then are willing to confess, repair, and live with the consequences. Second, yellow-light, or foolish, people are quick to say they are sorry but repeat the pattern again and again. Their behavior doesn't seem to change even if their initial emotional response looked like remorse. Finally, red-light people, or what the Bible calls evil people or wolves in sheep's clothing, are those who take joy in harming others, which also harms themselves. They experience no regret and are quick to defend their ways. Let's explore this further.[2]

THE GREEN-LIGHT, YELLOW-LIGHT, OR RED-LIGHT LEADER

Green-Light People

Green-light leaders are humans who make mistakes but are willing to take ownership and learn from those mistakes. They have good days and bad days, but when approached directly about the harm they did, they are open, responsive, and do not defend their behaviors. They see your honesty as helpful and might even appreciate it, making the relationship ultimately stronger. Though discussion is often needed, they are open to listening to your point of view and can sit with the hurts and effects of their behaviors. These leaders are not perfect, but they do demonstrate a heart that wants to be right with you and God, empathizing with the pain they caused (knowingly or unknowingly). They willingly confess and own their contributions without guilt, shame, or blame. They earnestly try to make the changes needed for the relationships to experience repair and to sustain trust.

It is still a risk to trust that someone's confession is sincere, but when you see these traits, there is hope for moving toward grieving, identifying the consequences, and eventually forgiveness. Reconciliation, requiring two participating parties, is the final step of healing and is possible with a wise person. Conflict is inevitable in relationships, but how one handles the conflict is what tells us whether he or she is a green-light person.

For example, one way I (Terra) see this play out in my relationship with Jeff is how he writes specific action steps following our conflicts. His method of choice is a sticky note he displays on our bathroom mirror, where we both can see it. Jeff's builder wiring appreciates clear direction and a way to move toward results. He channels that motivation with his sticky notes. He prayerfully considers those words daily. Is the change overnight? No. However, his heart and effort are in the right place: a posture of wanting to be right before God and with me. Jeff is known to do this with those in his sphere of influence as a way to be intentional in remaining a green-light leader.

Yellow-Light People

These people are known to be hot and cold. One moment they are for you, and the next moment you feel like you are walking on eggshells. It's hard to trust yellow-light people, yet it's often difficult to put a finger on the reason why. When approached with a concern or conflict, these leaders will become defensive and are skilled at minimizing the problem. When they do show remorese or other appropriate emotions, it's often out of the shame they feel of getting caught. They might intentionally shift the focus as a way to manipulate. At times, the yellow-light person will try to talk about the issues, but in the end there is no formal repair or lasting improvement.

Yellow-light people have little awareness of their internal world, and their identity is often rooted in their performance; hearing any feedback feels like an attack on their personhood. They may attempt to talk about the issues but quickly point to circumstances or other people, demanding evidence, and making all-or-nothing statements such as, "You are either on board or not." Yellow-light people are very skilled at justifying their behaviors, to the point of using Scripture. They say things like, "Everyone sins and falls short of the glory of God," or "You truly misunderstand my intentions." Finally, if a yellow-light person does show repentance and claims to own his or her behaviors, there is little-to-no consistent follow-through. It's hard to know where you stand with yellow-light leaders, as their own lack of confidence and security runs interference in every relationship. With a little bit of time, they are right back where they started.

It is risky to trust the words of a yellow-light person, and only time will tell whether his or her initial posture of remorse is sincere. The solution is to no longer have discussions and to begin to clearly articulate boundaries and next-step initiatives. Actions will speak louder than words with yellow-light people. You can continue to heal on your own, naming the behaviors, grieving the consequences and their impact on you, and eventually forgiving. However, restored relationship may not be possible, as trust is the foundation of every healthy relationship. Withholding full reconciliation until you see signs of consistent green-light patterns is key here. We caution against leaders being placed back into roles of greater influence if they demonstrate this pattern, as the wake of their destruction and the consequences of their choices only grow larger. This leader is the one who has harmed, possibly even taken steps toward ownership, but still wants the consequences to be dismissed or the processes to be rushed. These leaders are ready to share all they learned from their mistakes. This is truly part of the addiction cycle for these leaders and is easily missed in the greater church system. There is a short-lived period of time when what yellow-light people say matches what they do. As our friend Bill Thrall likes to say, their theology has not yet penetrated the reality of their life. It is most loving to give this kind of person a chance for an awakening experience that is sustained over time so trust can be rebuilt.

Red-Light People

These are the hardest people to understand. They are predators, wolves in sheep's clothing and not the burdened sinners they often seem. Red-light people envy you and want what you have, even to the point of intentionally hurting others. They see people as a means to an end, serving only themselves. They like to bring others down and create chaos within organizations. They are not willing to change, and they continue to make their victims feel like fools. With little to no remorse, they gain power by confusing the systems around them, gaining access to the vulnerable and earning the trust of decision makers, all with the purpose of doing harm. From the work we do, we have found it's difficult to help leaders—and those who follow them—identify this type of person.

We have sat with yellow-light people who confessed and found miraculous restoration because they submitted themselves to the process, owning and doing the needed repair work over a long period of time. But there are those who find themselves in the same cycle every one or two or three years. As Cloud said, it's the pattern, not a particular problem, that clues us in to the evil.[3] Especially in Christian circles, it's hard to believe that people would take delight in hurting and taking down marriages, families, organizations, and churches for their own benefit. We know God's power and grace can break through any hard heart, but the reality is, that's God's job—not ours. Recognizing the difference brings freedom.

When we realize we are dealing with a red-light person, that's the time to change strategies. Too often we ask human beings to take on the work by offering trite and naive suggestions: "Well, maybe if you obeyed, or you submitted, told them what you needed, or if you had more faith, or you said no." One has to shift from helping mode into protection mode in order for there to be any hopeful change on any level. Otherwise, more sheep are bound to be victimized. The more intense the situation, the greater the need for protection. Unpacking what protection looks like in each red-light relationship is vital. In some cases, this means bringing in trained professionals such as counselors, lawyers, police, and DHS, and even using restraining orders for there to be any chance for healing for the victims.

There is a distinct difference between people who confess to minimize the severity of the consequences they must suffer and those who genuinely let others see underneath their shame. Unfortunately, we have found that most confession comes after someone has been caught, rather than for the right reasons. It can take time and consistency to discern the difference. **When people wait to confess until after they are caught, confession can become a tool, a strategy to control the narrative and those affected.** People who truly want to be free in the way of James 5:16 (confessing and praying) likely already have a habit of letting others in. Our team at Living Wholehearted has listened to thousands of confessions from both Christian and non-Christian leaders and have come to understand that the initial disclosure is usually only the tip of the iceberg.

> There is a distinct difference between people who confess to minimize the severity of the consequences they must suffer and those who genuinely let others see underneath their shame.

After years and years of stuffing, hiding, lying, justifying, and more, the one confessing often becomes confused about truth. He no longer understands the whole truth and is rarely able to trust himself with it, let alone another human being. The confession process must be handled with great care, both for the confessor and for the victims who were violated and hurt along the way. The roles of compartmentalization (discussed in chapter 5) and dissociation should be considered when evaluating confessions of enormous gravity. By the time someone is caught, he usually has spent years compartmentalizing secrets (maybe even starting in childhood). We have compassion for this process but even more compassion for all those harmed by years of hiding.

If an aspect of integrity is being the same person behind closed doors as in public, then living with nothing hidden is the key to being a Wholehearted Leader. Why is voluntary authentic confession at any level so rare? We believe intense fear of the consequences keeps people from confessing. The trouble is that we generally do not live in environments of trust and grace, and we know the cost of our confession could be great. We see stories daily on the news, and most can recall a story or two from their own experience. In addition, a system that minimizes the work necessary after someone confesses enables the confessor to do as little as possible. The tragedy is that confessing truth and facing the consequences of our behavior are two critical markers on the path to healing, leading to peace of mind, body, and soul. There are no shortcuts. Consequently, those with less power (younger generations looking to climb the ranks) often reject the structures and systems that seemingly led to the downfall of other leaders, trying to shortcut their own corruption. **The root of hiding is a desire to avoid pain. Ironically, the root of confessing is also a desire to avoid pain. However, one leads to healing, while the other leads to a festering wound that kills from the inside out.**

Every leader needs to have a relationship of trust where he or she is fully honest. Sometimes the confidential space of a counseling office is the safest place to start, with the hope one practices for their real relationships.

STORIES OF RED-LIGHT PEOPLE

In 2005 Gallup launched a four-year study on why people follow leaders. Sampling more than ten thousand people, Gallup found that the four basic needs of followers are trust, compassion, stability, and hope.[4] There is a remarkable difference between good shepherds honoring these needs in their followers and poser-like shepherds— most likely with fragile egos—leveraging these real needs to their own advantage. Two recent cases in American society have shown leaders who took advantage of their followers' needs, got caught, and then dug in their heels to avoid confessing and facing the consequences. Let's study the cases of a fraudulent financial investor and the forty-second president of the United States.

Bernie Madoff, the former nonexecutive chairman of the NASDAQ stock market, confessed to running the largest Ponzi scheme ever. Prosecutors estimated the fraud to be $64.8 billion based on Madoff's November 2008 report to his 4,800 clients just before the scheme was discovered. Although Madoff told authorities he began his scheme in the 1990s, federal investigators believe it began in the 1970s, possibly even earlier.[5]

In December 2008, Madoff's sons, who worked for him, alerted authorities that their father had confessed that his investment advisory business was a massive Ponzi scheme. They quoted him as saying it was "just one big lie."[6] It's hard to imagine what it was like to be a son of Bernie Madoff in that moment. In one glaring instant, the father who provided the structure that had met your family's needs your entire life confessed that his contributions were a big lie and you were part of the fraud. Thousands of people lost their entire savings—money put away for retirement, college tuition, and critical medicine and surgeries. Two years later, one son committed suicide, and in 2014 the other passed away from lymphoma. Today Madoff sits in federal prison serving a maximum sentence of one hundred fifty years.

On Madoff's sentencing date in 2009, he apologized to his victims, saying, "I have left a legacy of shame, as some of my victims have pointed out, to my family and my grandchildren. That's something I will live with for the rest of my life.… I am sorry."[7] Judge Denny Chin, who oversaw the case, had not received any letters from friends or family telling of Madoff's good deeds. "The absence of such support is telling," he said. Judge Chin also faulted Madoff for *not* being forthcoming about his crimes, calling the fraud "extraordinarily evil," "unprecedented," and "staggering." He hoped the sentence would deter others from committing similar frauds.[8]

Serving a life prison sentence did not deter Bernie Madoff from reversing course from his alleged remorse for the shame he had brought to his family and grandchildren. In 2015, just six years later, he sought to reframe the public's opinion of himself and his actions by asserting in an email, "The facts were that the majority of my individual clients were net winners." An article from CNBC in 2015 explains that while Madoff tried to place the attention on the monies recovered, he refused to address the billions of dollars in returns that his clients were promised but which never materialized.[9] Over time the reality of Madoff's heart was revealed despite how sincere his public apology seemed in 2009. As we were editing this book, Madoff was in the news again, trying to manipulate the public to pressure decision-makers for an early release from prison due to alleged health issues. Think, *red-light person.*

Perhaps an even more well-known story of a leader with predatory behaviors is that of Bill Clinton. His affair with then White House intern Monica Lewinsky began in 1995, during his first term as president, but didn't become public until 1998. Clinton famously lied to the American people when he asserted during a nationally televised press conference that he "did not have sexual relations with that woman." He repeatedly denied the relationship before later admitting to "inappropriate intimate physical contact" with Lewinsky. The House of Representatives impeached the president for perjury and obstruction of justice, but he was acquitted by the Senate.[10]

During what became an exhausting saga in the news cycle for more than a year, Clinton spoke publicly about his motivations for concealing his affair:

> I know that my public comments and my silence about this matter gave a false impression. I misled people, including even my wife. I deeply regret that.
>
> I can only tell you I was motivated by many factors. First, by a desire to protect myself from the embarrassment of my own conduct. I was also very concerned about protecting my family....
>
> In addition, I had real and serious concerns about an independent counsel investigation that began with private business dealings twenty years ago, dealings, I might add, about which an independent federal agency found no evidence of any wrongdoing by me or my wife over two years ago.
>
> The independent counsel investigation moved on to my staff and friends, then into my private life. And now the investigation itself is under investigation.
>
> This has gone on too long, cost too much and hurt too many innocent people.[11]

Although "Clinton's growing-up years were spent in a home with an alcoholic stepfather who was violent, abusive, and unfaithful to his mother," he maintained his personal perception of a "normal childhood."[12] This is a common narrative of adults in denial of their childhood pain. Ruth Haley Barton, a spiritual director, discussed Clinton's road to confession in her book on spiritual leadership: "Apparently, Clinton's ability to deny what was real and to describe his childhood as something it was not developed at an early age, and it helped him survive psychologically. It is what he needed to believe in order to cope with his situation; however, the long-term result was that he developed unconscious patterns of denial that did not serve him well as an adult and as a leader.... He was likable but he was not trustworthy."[13]

It's been more than a decade since Bernie Madoff was sentenced and more than two decades since Bill Clinton was impeached in the House of Representatives. Ironically, both Madoff and Clinton were recently in the news—less than a few weeks apart—still trying to manipulate the public perception. Behind bars, Madoff continues to try to control the historical narrative that got him a life sentence, and similarly, Bill and Hillary Clinton still attempt to control the public narrative about them and their past. In the documentary *Hillary*, Clinton blamed his choices for the affair with Lewinsky on his anxiety.[14] As we write this, Bill and Hillary Clinton are seemingly being shut out of the limelight by the Democratic Party that used to put them on the highest pedestal. It's as if the party cannot afford to cover for or use the Clintons any longer because their past has had a negative impact on the image the party wants to portray to the American people. *(By the way, this is not a political statement. The Clintons are only one example of thousands.)*

Being charismatic, capable, and likable does not equate to being trustworthy. We must all be aware that we are vulnerable to being used by leaders and the systems they create. Jesus, who knew that people were not to be elevated in such a way, "would not entrust himself to [the people], for he knew all people. He did not need any testimony about mankind, for he knew what was in each person" (John 2:24–25).

Freedom comes at a price. If we want to experience freedom from the sins we find ourselves entangled in (no matter how we got there), we have to address our part squarely through ongoing rhythms of soul care, confession, and repentance. We often think of what seems to come naturally for children; they do not need to be taught to hide wrongdoing. It has been part of our nature since the fall in Genesis 3, when Adam and Eve tried to hide behind fig leaves. The propensity of our sinful nature—our default from birth to death—is to self-protect and hide in order to control our narrative and that of our world. This is true of everyone —from the slightest sins of a child to the Madoffs and Clintons of the world, whose actions carry high stakes and cause enormous ripple effects.

A PERSONAL STORY

(Jeff) We understand that the art of hiding starts when we are small and can be reinforced or shifted. When our younger daughter, Nevie, was in preschool, she got ahold of a bag of my favorite Christmas cookies I had stashed in the freezer. (I planned to enjoy them as long as possible!) Terra began looking for our daughter, calling out to her with no response. Thinking she might be hiding, she quietly entered Nevie's bedroom and opened the closet doors. She found Nevie crouched in the corner, holding the empty cookie bag with only greasy fingers and a few crumbs to spare. When she was found, she chose to stop hiding and admit her wrongdoing. With Mom's guidance, she took the next steps of repentance by asking for forgiveness, receiving forgiveness, and feeling the warm hug of acceptance from both her parents, reassuring her that she was going to be okay. Since our daughter was only in preschool, we celebrated her choice to confess (even though the evidence was clearly pointing to her!). The consequences, in her case, were small: an upset tummy and a lesson in asking for help instead of hiding.

SHRINKING THIS GAP

Confession is not just for our homes; it's for our workplaces too. Some of you may be laughing at the thought of confessing anything to anyone at work. To do such a thing could look weak or give ammunition to be used against you. We can pretend that hiding our wrongdoings is a helpful alternative (saving face, our jobs, our pride) and is not hurting anyone. We may even convince ourselves that it is actually better, as Clinton shared in later remarks. "The heart is deceitful above all things" (Jer. 17:9). **Leaders who operate from unhealthy motives are clever at justifying their desire to hide and learning to spin the narratives so their sheep will feel the blame.** These maladaptive coping strategies are built over years, and until others in the system start to detect them earlier, we will continue dealing with the wake of disaster in our organizations and families.

Of course, the biblical truth that the human heart is vulnerable to creating and propagating deception, is in direct opposition to one of the primary messages that popular media feeds to children and families today: "Follow your heart." This message, combined with actual trauma, shapes some of the maladaptive coping strategies that yellow-light and red-light leaders use. Many wise parents are helping their children discern the subtle (and sometimes not so subtle) lies in the movies, music, and television shows that dominate the entertainment and educational landscapes today. God help us there! It's not about protecting them and others *from* anymore; it's about protecting *through* everything that inundates them today.

How can we normalize confession at every step of our journeys? For Christians, this means a regular rhythm of confession. No actual healing can come without confession. Whether one follows Jesus or not, letting another into our *entire* story is healing; we are hardwired to be known. In fact, before we at Living Wholehearted move into the presenting issues of a client, it is standard practice to do a time line of the client's story. Simply telling our narratives invites us to experience feeling exposed but not ashamed. The counseling office limits the consequences, and the confidentiality provides a sense of protection, which is why our counseling offices are filled every day. Yet any good therapy will help a client move to face consequences at some point in his or her journey. **The key is having grace-filled help to not hide, ignore, minimize, dismiss, or rationalize away the wrong done to oneself or others out of one's own pain.**

One of the most sobering and repeated storylines in our offices is of the high-capacity Christian leader who tells a victim of abuse, or a spouse of an addict, to forgive the offender and repair the relationship with that person. **Leaders have an unhealthy tendency to advise people to rush the repair process before there is ever grief, remorse, or recognition of the hurt. Even if the offender does**

confess, the consequence may be the extended time that survivors need to heal before relationship is even a possibility.

Often confession in a family or organizational system means consequences for everyone, not just the offending party. In one of our counseling narratives, the wife was never told by senior leadership that her husband, a pastor on staff, was having serial affairs. The church helped conceal his actions until years later, when the wife was in the same situation at another church and someone finally spoke up. For twenty-five years she thought the issue was her not forgiving her husband. Her healing today is related not only to her ex-husband, who still defends his years of sex addiction, but also to the many church leaders who did not help them and instead looked to control the narrative. The cost of doing confession well is time consuming and financially burdensome, and it means we must dive deeper into the pain—actually touch the bleeding woman (see chap. 8; Mark 5).

Confession can cost us all, but as leaders, it is essential that we do our own work so we can help others discern and take steps toward healing and wholeness. We know (many personally) followers of Jesus in every nation on earth who still take God at His Word and trust His heart for them. We beg you to keep going in God's strength as you regularly confess, repent, forgive, receive forgiveness, and grow in your desire to think, love, and live like Christ. Daniel, an example of a righteous leader in the Old Testament, spent regular time confessing, giving thanks, and asking for the restoration of his people (see Dan. 6:10; 9:15–19).

When we understand that our position as believers is sealed the day we accept Jesus as our Lord and Savior, we become the very righteousness of Christ. Something inside us shifts, and we no longer need to prove ourselves righteous by our behavior. In fact, it frees us up to admit when we are wrong, because we no longer connect our identity to our behavior. We can breathe deeply and find freedom in saying out loud what we wrestle with inside. It's powerful and inspiring to see people (young or old) trusting their identity in Jesus and following His lead, even when they err in their humanity. Just as Jesus changed the environments He stepped into by His words and actions, so do His followers who think, love, and act like Him. God reveals Himself through His children in every environment all around the world.

IN THE BIBLE

Jesus said, "If you love me, obey my commandments" (John 14:15 NLT). He wasn't just talking about the Ten Commandments. He was talking about keeping in step with His indwelling presence in our lives, allowing His transforming power to change us from the inside out. Christian leaders, in particular, are to be like Jesus in public spaces. But the *only* way we can maintain this standard in the public sphere is to be committed to it in private also. **Confession should happen regularly in both spaces. It reduces hiddenness and directs our energy to becoming more whole and available to actually love others.** In *The Message*, James 5:15–16 says,

> Believing-prayer will heal you, and Jesus will put you on your feet. And if you've sinned, you'll be forgiven—healed inside and out.

> Make this your common practice: Confess
> your sins to each other and pray for each other so
> that you can live together whole and healed. The
> prayer of a person living right with God is some-
> thing powerful to be reckoned with.

(Terra) I recently confessed to my dear friend that I was wrong in the way I spoke to her. Though I could justify it based on my stress levels, my hormones, my pain, and the context, the fact was, I was wrong. Period. She did not deserve to be spoken to that way, and I surely do not want to hurt her. Giving my friend a chance to respond to my request for forgiveness was vital to the process. She may not have been ready to forgive me and needed some time. In honoring that time, I would have shown her that my repentance was sincere. However, she was ready and formally let go so we both could move forward. Being perfect is not the key to integrity. Rather, we must practice recognizing when we are veering from integrity.

Those who came before Jesus' public ministry knew that God created and required confession and repentance. They understood that God gave these disciplines because they were good for those He created in His image. John the Baptist heard people's confessions before baptizing them in the Jordan River (see Matt. 3:5–6). The Psalms give readers a glimpse of the intimate honesty David shared with God, functioning like his journal entries and exposing his thoughts, feelings, and desires. One of David's finest hours came after his gravest sins when he could no longer live with himself. David felt the weight of his choices in his body and soul. (If we actually pay attention, so can we.) Reflecting on this, David wrote,

Blessed is the one whose transgression is forgiven,
>   whose sin is covered.
Blessed is the man against whom the LORD counts
>   no iniquity,
>   and in whose spirit there is no deceit.

For when I kept silent, my bones wasted away
>   through my groaning all day long.
For day and night your hand was heavy upon me;
>   my strength was dried up as by the heat of
>   summer.

I acknowledged my sin to you,
>   and I did not cover my iniquity;
I said, "I will confess my transgressions to the
>   LORD,"
>   and you forgave the iniquity of my sin.
>   (Ps. 32:1–5 ESV)

God knew that David needed to be cleansed from his sin in order to be free from burden and bondage. He sent David a trusted spiritual leader, mentor, and friend named Nathan to help him expose what he was trying to hide (see 2 Sam. 12). As you may know, David was not spared consequences just because he chose to confess, and part of what made David a man after God's heart (1 Sam. 13:14; Acts 13:22) is that he did not try to manage the consequences. He received forgiveness and trusted the difficult process. David and his wife lost the son she gave birth to, and David grieved the loss. Even in the midst of these traumatic events, David's confession to the Lord and to a trusted person led to him knowing and feeling true freedom.

When we start trusting God's ways and stop trying to control outcomes, we become leaders after God's heart. Many have lived a regular rhythm of confession and kept the reins tight—Daniel and Joseph, to name a couple. In the same psalm, David reflected this posture: "Let all the faithful pray to you while you may be found; surely the rising of the mighty waters will not reach them. You are my hiding place; you will protect me from trouble and surround me with songs of deliverance" (Ps. 32:6–7). He went on to record one of the most important truths found in the Bible: "The LORD's unfailing love surrounds the one who trusts in him" (v. 10). What is your trust level with God? With others? We cannot give what we don't have.

If the consequences of confessing your sins (loss of respect, job, marriage, wealth, dignity, etc.) terrify you, consider the fact that there are no shortcuts to the lasting peace and freedom you seek. In fact, the reason you are hiding in a closet—shoving cookies in your mouth—is probably that you have an unmet need that God is so ready to meet if you will let Him. God Himself provided a way for you (created in His very image) to be free from the burdens you carry.

The unforced rhythms of grace include confession. Unburden yourself, but we advise doing it in wisdom and with a trusted person—either someone you respect, like Nathan in David's story, or a counselor.

THE CALL

We are calling for a revolutionary change by emerging leaders who are ready to lead from a different path—not an easy one, but one followers of Jesus are called to walk. Rather than running into the light and saying, "I did it," we have a compulsion to pull away and hide in shame. When we walk closely with God and others, our internal compass will tell us when something is wrong. It's what we do in those moments that makes all the difference. No matter our age or worldview, the propensity to hide is innate. It takes courage, intention, and God's help to voluntarily bring things forward into the light, own our part, take time to repair (if possible), and practically commit to doing things in honesty. His grace is always ready to receive us, forgive our wrongdoings, and restore our sense of self, yet grace does not exempt us from the consequences of our choices. Too many of us have avoided being found or confessing until the consequences are so high the wall seems unscalable.

If the fear of confessing and losing everything keeps us imprisoned, Satan, our and God's Enemy, is happy to let us stay there. We learn from Jesus that Satan's singular focus, as long as he is allowed to have influence in this world, is to "steal and kill and destroy" like a thief in the night. In contrast, Jesus tells us that He came so we "may have life, and have it to the full" (John 10:10).

Through the sacrifice of God's Son, Jesus, sin does not separate us from the goodness of God. In short, Jesus paid a great price to save us all eternally and offer us wholeness right here and now. Belief in God's plan for our salvation through Jesus does not protect us from choosing to sin (oh, how we wish it did) and experiencing sin's heavy burden. However, He did provide a way out. Confessing our sin to God and to another trusted person releases us from the bondage of sin. It takes time and consistency to prevent that sin from creeping back in. Being human means the neuropathways in our brains are patterned after our ways of being in the world, and we need new experiences over a consistent period of time to see long-lasting change in our minds, bodies, and souls. The immediate release of our confession is powerful, but facing the consequences, grieving, owning, sitting with those we harmed (if doing so will not harm them more), and choosing a new way again and again is what changes us from the inside out: mileage confirming our confessions and repentant hearts. The process is slower than we like, especially in a Western culture that adores quick, easy, and the ability to wipe out our online histories with a click.

Confession is the gateway to the narrow road that Jesus said only a few will travel (see Matt. 7:14). Our commitment to taking the journey of repentance (a turning of all our ways) means that we choose to walk a different direction (with the help of another) and learn a new way of being from that point forward. Facing the impact of our choices is part of the new path. Telling others it's over and you are changed, asking why they cannot forgive you, or hoping the press will die down is a sign of controlling the consequences and not of true repentance. True repentance means we may need to take a longer walk with those we've harmed. As our friends at Trueface say, "Grace is not soft on sin."[15]

> True repentance means we may need to take a longer walk with those we've harmed.

In other words, the grace of Jesus Christ is only available to us because He suffered and died to provide it. There is no get-out-of-jail-free card. A price was paid, and Jesus requires us to acknowledge, in recognition of His grace, the sin we have committed. When He gave His famous Sermon on the Mount and said, "Blessed are those who mourn, for they will be comforted" (Matt. 5:4), the mourning He was talking about was grief over our sin. Joseph Stowell put it this way: "It means that kingdom people are blessed when they experience mourning deep inside because of the tragic nature of their sinfulness and its consequences, its deep offense to God, and its negative impact on the lives of those around them."[16] In coming face to face with the goodness of God, we are humbled to know how loved we are despite the wrong we do.

Our love for our daughter Nevie never wavered when she was caught with the empty cookie bag. Yet our relationship with her, and her with us, was built on honesty and trust from that point on. This ongoing pattern of confession in our home is to prepare our girls to live as leaders of integrity who are sensitive to the grace of God, His love for them and others, and their utter need to stay close to His heart. Our confession to them when we've wronged them is to keep it real.

To willfully hide and hold a habit of sinning (whatever it is) while professing to follow Jesus is a heavy burden to bear. We trust your bones are aching, and if they aren't, then you might have become too accustomed to living with the pain. Every one of us has felt the longing to be free when we find ourselves entangled in sin. The unfailing love of our God made a way for us, a path for us to walk that guarantees our freedom, even as we face consequences in this life for our sins. If you truly love God, then choose again and again and again to obey His commands. When you are struggling, confess to someone and seek help. When we choose confession, we gain something more precious than anything—peace with God and assurance that He is with us and for us and will never leave us. There is no substitute for this peace with God, and no one but God can provide it. We trust Him to. We have seen Him do so in the most devastating situations.

Romans 8:31–39 says there is nothing that can separate us from the love of God—and that means nothing. It is through His Holy Spirit that people can face the consequences of their sins and still thrive. Not all relationships will be repaired or restored. However, how we approach confession of our sins is vital to whether there is a chance. Despite our fears and the lies we tell ourselves, the truth is that **if we do not confess, we will lose everything! It's just a matter of time.**

Key Markers of Hiding

- In times of great distress, you avoid people who know you well.
- You try to manage consequences or defend your reasoning for decisions.
- Your body feels the cost of hiding and the fear of being found out (evident in anxiety, depression, etc.).
- You make decisions based on a narrative you think you control, and you work hard to keep control of that narrative.
- You overpower or push away those who try to question you, even if they are trying to help you.

- You are skilled at minimizing, deflecting, scapegoating, and overpowering, even to the point of believing your own lies.

Antidotes

1. Name what you have been hiding. Write down everything that is weighing you down, big or small. Start by trusting God with your confession. Next, find a trusted friend, counselor, or mentor who can help you take further steps as needed.

2. Consider a team to help you move through confession, repentance, and repair in order to not do more harm along the way. Once you confess, you might feel relieved, as you have been living with a hidden life (many report just how good confession feels). However, those hearing the confession for the first time will likely be directly affected and may need time to process a new reality and the costs of your wrongdoing. They may need the help of trusted friends, mentors, and professional counselors themselves.

3. Depending on the gravity of your confession, consider what you might lose and the consequences you might face when you tell someone. This exercise helps you prepare for letting go and facing the realities associated with the wrongdoing you committed. *Anything* you do not lose through confession and repentance is yours by grace alone. Remember, there is no shortcut to actual freedom. Full confession and repentance are always required for experiencing the freedom that almost all guilty people want for their hearts, minds, bodies, and souls. Let God, and the complete freedom only He can

provide, be your motivation to walk the difficult path of confession and repentance. If you keep your eyes on God and commit to following His ways, you can be sure He will be with you, even if it feels as though no one else is.

4. Practice lamenting. This means grieving for your own and others' sins. We have created a culture that delights only in what feels good. Take time to practice attuning your heart to what breaks God's heart. A great place to start is praying through the Psalms, where David did this very thing.

5. Journal. Consider daily and weekly rhythms of confession to keep your heart, mind, body, and relationships pure. The discipline of smaller confessions can help us stay on track and focused on what really matters.

Conclusion

HOPE FOR WHOLEHEARTED LEADERSHIP

The thing about sheep is they have a tendency to focus on the grass that's right in front of them. Therefore, someone has to keep an eye on where the flock is going.... Someone has to keep an eye on the horizon to see where the green grass is. That person also has to keep the flock together and lead it where it needs to go.

—Kevin Leman and William Pentak, *The Way of the Shepherd*

We did not write this book to add to the stream of tweets, posts, and headlines pointing to any particular leader's famous rise and fall. Our perspective on the integrity gap comes from nearly two decades of sitting behind the closed doors of counseling and coaching offices. We definitely did not want to write this book on some high seat of judgment as if we are without flaw or have perfectly achieved integrity ourselves. We wrote it because, like you, we have been deeply grieved by this broken record being played everywhere we turn, especially its surge within the Christian church. We know we are not alone.

We began by defining a leader in the simplest manner. You are a leader if you have someone following you. **Whether one or millions follow you, how you live and lead matters.** We defined integrity as a commitment to continuing to shrink the gap between the values you preach and the values you actually practice. For leaders, integrity is a process of allowing ourselves to be human, learning to live and lead with greater congruence and grace rather than from behind a title and its inherent power. We are saying that **integrity is not just a word; it's a way of being.** We asked you to imagine leadership where you are actually seen, known, even loved, and then, from that place of authenticity, be able to offer the same to those you influence.

Whether you profess to be a Christian leader or not, you and everyone you influence benefits when you wake up to the importance of shrinking your integrity gap. The converse is also true. Everyone in your leadership wake (especially you) pays when your gap grows … it's only a matter of time. In fact, we may not see all the fruit of our investment in this endeavor; it will likely be our children's children who experience the full impact.

The toxic symptoms of leadership we've detailed (unresolved trauma, triggers, shame, narcissism, burnout, isolation, hiding, etc.) can create wiggle room for moral failures to creep into any movement or institution—government, education, business, or religion. No system is exempt. We all long for shepherds, to have people in charge who will solve our problems and the larger problems in the world. However when we ignore our leaders' personal lives, looking only at what they do for us, sheep remain vulnerable—very vulnerable.

We have listened to high-level leaders inside and outside the Christian faith share their trauma and the ways they thought they could overcome or hide it. For so many leaders, achievement was their way of dealing with trauma. What many discover years later is that their trauma has been leaking all along. It spills over the walls they built to keep it in the past. Consequently, the trauma-tized perpetrate trauma on others and never see it happening until something snaps.

The toxic trend of Christian leaders rising to celebrity sta-tus and falling from influence, authority, and credibility must change if the church is to be trusted. The Bible calls God's church the bride of Christ, and He—and we—still love her, even with all her blemishes. We know that the wisdom shared here will not save—only Christ can. However, we do believe that we are to steward a gift we have been given through our own losses and those we have walked so intimately with over the years. We still believe in the noble pursuit of shrinking our integrity gaps. In every generation since the beginning of time, there has been a remnant who have also said, "Enough is enough; it's time for a change." You can be a part of this!

HOPE FOR CHRISTIAN LEADERS

As we embrace our identity as heirs of the King of Kings and invite God to help us close our personal and corporate integrity gaps, we honor Jesus with our whole selves. Wholehearted Leaders honor Him not just with our words, our minds, our hearts, or our bod-ies for an hour on Sundays but with all of who we are in private and public. As our gaps shrink, we grow closer to experiencing our God-given potential, both personally and corporately, and everyone benefits, even those who do not profess to follow Jesus. We spend less time and energy healing and more energy living the lives God intended for us. In fact, when we have done our own work, it becomes easier to enter into the hardships of others with the utmost humility and grace. In this way, we become part of the answer to the prayer Jesus taught us to pray to our Father in heaven: "Your kingdom come, your will be done, on earth as it is in heaven" (Matt. 6:10). This is a desire He wants us to have—and a reality He wants to partner with us on.

In the sanctification process, we submit ourselves to God as saints (who still sin), saved by grace through faith. This journey of faith is complete only when we meet our Maker. In this lifetime we would be wise to remember that "faith is what faith does."[1] Here the gap closes between what Christians preach and what they actually live out. Good shepherds are submitted to the Great Shepherd, Jesus Christ. **As they submit themselves on a daily basis to God and a trusted community, they stay in His light, depend on Him to meet their needs, and repair when necessary rather than try to hide.**

As the world experiences more Christian leaders living and leading authentically with greater humility and integrity (not perfection), better balancing truth and grace, we believe that more people outside the faith will "taste and see that the LORD is good" (Ps. 34:8). They will believe and choose to follow Him because they saw Him, heard Him, and felt Him in a leader who was like Him (a good shepherd).

If you are a leader who rose only to fall, please imagine with us once again! God has not forgotten you. He has not abandoned you. No one can disqualify you from what He wills to do in and through you except yourself. He will not violate your will, yet He is inviting you, turning toward you, longing for you to run back to Him and His ways. Your greatest contribution may yet be in helping this and the next generation of emerging leaders understand the wisdom you learned from your journey and mentoring them in how to shrink their integrity gaps sooner and then sustain integrity until they finish their assignments on this earth.

D. L. Moody once said, "Most people talk cream, and live skim milk."[2] We have a few friends who do not identify as Christians but who talk skim and live cream better than most Christians we know. Brothers and sisters, this should not be! Will you be the one to set the example for other believers (and those yet to believe) in your sphere of influence in speech, life, love, faith, and purity, as the apostle Paul challenged his protégé Timothy (see 1 Tim. 4:12)? You cannot do this on your own. Did you catch that? But God can do it through you if you let Him!

The only way to become a Wholehearted Leader is to learn to trust and cling to God and a few safe people through His Holy Spirit. From the foundation of trust in God comes the beautiful freedom to integrate your faith into action more and more. This freedom arrives after we choose to trust that God has received our confession, removed our guilt, and sent us off to play again and be about His kingdom work right here, right now. This freedom grows when we look back to when we were younger and where we may have received an early trauma that affects our way of relating to God and others. Leaders need to take the time as early as possible in their journey to do the hard work of letting God, wise mentors, and counselors (good shepherds) help them identify, understand, and truly heal from early traumas. When you dismiss your trauma and in turn look to others to meet unmet needs, the cycle of trauma is again perpetrated on others. But healing allows you to redirect that energy to serving others without expecting anything in return.

As Christian leaders, we practically integrate our faith into action even more as we embrace the humility Jesus modeled for us. This means accepting who God says He is along with who God says we are as His children: righteous, loved, forgiven, redeemed, known, significant, destined. We crave this wholeness, whether or not we identify ourselves as Christians, because that's how we all were designed to live. Start by asking God for help. Then take one step forward. Our Maker knows which path each of us must walk, by our own free will, because He created us and the path. He will be with us every step of the way (whether we feel Him near or not).

Most leaders, as a type, have some level of narcissistic tendencies. Remember that compartmentalization leaves us living and leading from a false reality. High-capacity leaders can lose the ability to discern between their perceived reality and actual reality. It's essential to stay in touch with reality through real, life-giving relationships that provide accountability. Because too many leaders live and lead with narcissistic personality disorder (diagnosed or not), leaders and followers alike must become more aware of and educated about it so we do not participate in promoting this abuse. Practice confession and being known for who you are as a person, not for your title or what you do. Invite regular feedback into your life. Look for spiritually mature people who do not need anything from you and are emotionally in a place where they enjoy the freedom to give to others.

HOPE IN THE CHURCH

The Christian church can lead this needed change. Ministry must no longer be a safe haven where leaders can rise in power and influence while they hide, abuse, and seek to meet their selfish needs at the expense of others. We are encouraged by more and more Christian churches, organizations, businesses, and communities taking stands against predatory leaders. They are removing them from leadership, owning whatever parts are theirs to own in the abusive cycles, and helping to create systems, policies, and environments that will deter future abuse (God willing). Not all leaders on the spectrum of NPD are evil, are unable to be saved, or need to be banished from the church. No, Christ died for them, and His grace is sufficient for them as well (see 2 Cor. 12:9). Instead, we urge the church and the world to be better educated on how NPD forms in early childhood, the consequences of people living out their behavioral disorder throughout their lifespan, and how NPD can be managed so that those with it can contribute and be healthy, receiving members of a community. It may be hard for a rich person to enter the kingdom of heaven (see Matt. 19:24). It may be even harder for NPD leaders because so few are able to see themselves as having actually done wrong in God's or anyone else's eyes. Good thing God is a gracious, merciful, and perfect judge!

As a Christian leader, you integrate your faith and action as you learn to lean into the contributions you were created to make while at the same time learning to lean into the contributions others were created to make. Accepting our limitations and partnering with others grows our sense of destiny, especially as equal members of the body of Christ. With a motive to serve, honor, and empower others like Christ, take time to educate yourself on how people are differently wired and how their wiring works. Grow in listening skills and emotional intelligence. We make up God's family.

We were created differently but with the same purpose: to live in, through, and for God and to enjoy Him forever! How will you shrink your integrity gap as a Christian leader who likely has said "I believe everyone is uniquely created by God" but also lives and leads in a manner that communicates "I'd prefer you do things my way"? The man famous for coining the phrase *servant-leadership*, Robert Greenleaf, created what he called the acid test for servant-leadership. "How do you tell a servant-leader is at work? 'Do the people around the person grow?'"[3]

Wise leaders recognize that people flourish when they gather, when decisions are based on several perspectives, when activities and work allow all four core value types (Merchants, Bankers, Builders, and Innovators) to be seen and honored and to reach their potential. By embracing others and integrating them into your leadership, you reduce your chance of falling into the dangerous trap of isolation with its inevitable fallout. As you more frequently value the wisdom of others and their contributions to your life and leadership, you will likely come to enjoy the give-and-take of healthy relationship. This allows you to see others for who they truly are, making it safe for them to share their weaknesses and shrink their gaps too. The ripple effect is enormous, likely larger than you can imagine.

Our stories—trauma and all—do not have to define us or dictate our decisions. Like Joseph, who kept his eyes on the One who created him despite the betrayals, suffering, and temptations he endured, we can be leaders who live with integrity. Joseph experienced many moments when the trauma of being abandoned, abused, and used by his brothers could have dictated his choices. Instead, he said no to sleeping with his boss's wife (as she threw herself at him and then called him the bad guy), kept from seeking revenge on his brothers when they returned for food during a famine, and resisted using his power to get his needs met. Joseph submitted himself to his God. He was by no means perfect in his journey, but he let himself feel, he set boundaries, and he chose to trust his God with his life (see Gen. 37–47). Integrity is possible!

> Our stories—trauma and all—do not have to define us or dictate our decisions.

Choose to invite those in your wake to join you on your mission, and all will flourish! The physical, emotional, and spiritual energy you used to waste on negative pursuits (maintaining image, achieving, receiving earthly rewards, wearing masks, hiding, defending, and self-promoting) can instead be designated for real kingdom callings. All can be devoted to serving, loving, repairing, empowering, and pointing others to the only Leader deserving of our worship, our submission, and our devotion—the One to whom all glory, power, and honor is to be given. The One at whose name every knee shall bow and every tongue confess that He is Lord: Jesus (see Phil. 2:10–11).

May this truth inspire us: if we have a following, how we live and lead matters!

Now to him who is able to do immeasurably more than all we ask or imagine, according to his power that is at work within us, to him be glory in the church and in Christ Jesus throughout all generations, for ever and ever! Amen. (Eph. 3:20–21)

ACKNOWLEDGMENTS

To our mentors, teachers, and friends who have taken the time to know us and lean deep into our stories. We could not be here without you.

To the Living Wholehearted team, who are on the frontlines of helping leaders live with integrity.

To our church family, Rolling Hills Community Church.

To Michael Covington and the David C Cook team, who took a risk on us and have fanned the flame of this message! We love this tribe.

Appendix A

FAMILY GENOGRAM SAMPLE

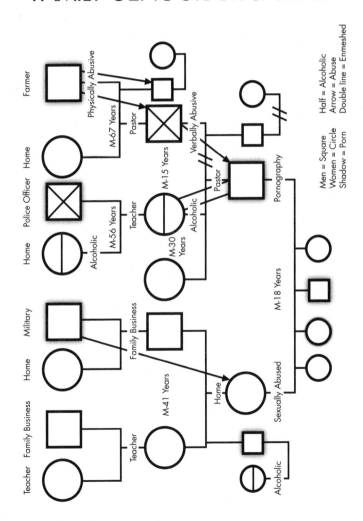

CONCENTRIC CIRCLES EXERCISE

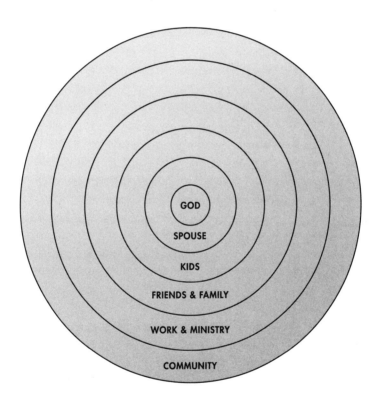

NOTES

INTRODUCTION

1. C. S. Lewis, "Is Theology Poetry?," in *"The Weight of Glory" and Other Addresses* (New York: HarperOne, 2001), 140.

2. Bill Thrall, Bruce McNicol, and Ken McElrath, *The Ascent of a Leader: How Ordinary Relationships Develop Extraordinary Character and Influence* (San Francisco: Jossey-Bass, 1999), 14.

CHAPTER 1: FOUNDATIONS OF LEADING

1. Parker J. Palmer, *A Hidden Wholeness: The Journey toward an Undivided Life* (San Francisco: Jossey-Bass, 2004), 8.

2. *Merriam-Webster*, s.v. "lead," www.merriam-webster.com/dictionary/lead.

3. Dave Jolly, quoted in David Brooks, *The Road to Character* (New York: Random House, 2015), xv.

4. Carol Wiley, "The Advantages of Compound Interest," Chron.com, https://smallbusiness.chron.com/advantages-compound-interest-20976.html.

5. James M. Kouzes and Barry Z. Posner, *Credibility: How Leaders Gain and Lose It, Why People Demand It*, rev. ed. (San Francisco: Jossey-Bass, 2011), xi.

CHAPTER 2: STORIES OF LEADING

1. Steven R. Tracy, *Mending the Soul: Understanding and Healing Abuse* (Grand Rapids, MI: Zondervan, 2005), 18.

2. Tracy, *Mending the Soul*, 43.

3. Desmond Tutu, *No Future without Forgiveness* (New York: Doubleday, 2000), 31.

4. *Diagnostic and Statistical Manual of Mental Disorders*, 5th ed. (Washington, DC: American Psychiatric Association, 2013).

5. Bessel van der Kolk, *The Body Keeps the Score: Brain, Mind, and Body in the Healing of Trauma* (New York: Penguin Books, 2015).

6. Brené Brown, *Daring Greatly: How the Courage to Be Vulnerable Transforms the Way We Live, Love, Parent, and Lead* (New York: Avery, 2012), 75.

7. Brené Brown would ask us to watch her epic empathy video at that point. "Brené Brown on Empathy," RSA, video, 2:53, December 10, 2013, www.youtube.com/watch?v=1Evwgu369Jw.

8. Celinne Da Costa, "The Millennial Workforce Needs Mentors, Not Managers," *Forbes*, May 25, 2018, www.forbes.com/sites/celinnedacosta/2018/05/25/the -millennial-workforce-needs-mentors-not-managers/#4ba23b68127a.

CHAPTER 3: TRAUMA AND TRIGGERS

1. Dan Allender, "Ambivalence and Our Wounded Hearts, Part One," podcast, February 25, 2017, https://theallendercenter.org/2017/02/ambivalence -wounded-hearts-1.

2. John Lynch, Bruce McNicol, and Bill Thrall, *The Cure: What If God Isn't Who You Think He Is and Neither Are You?*, 3rd ed. (Phoenix: Trueface, 2016), 47.

3. Curt Thompson, *Anatomy of the Soul: Surprising Connections between Neuroscience and Spiritual Practices That Can Transform Your Life and Relationships* (Carol Stream, IL: Tyndale, 2010), 83.

4. Thompson, *Anatomy of the Soul*, 4.

5. Paraphrase based on a story from Ruth Haley Barton, *Strengthening the Soul of Your Leadership: Seeking God in the Crucible of Ministry.* Copyright © 2008, 2018 by Ruth Haley Barton. Used by permission of InterVarsity Press, P.O. Box 1400, Downers Grove, IL 60515 USA. www.ivpress.com.

6. Barton, *Strengthening the Soul*, 55–56.

7. Barton, *Strengthening the Soul*, 63, 67.

8. Barton, *Strengthening the Soul*, 36–38, 55.

CHAPTER 4: GUILT AND TOXIC SHAME

1. Tristen Collins and Jonathan Collins, *Why Emotions Matter: Recognize Your Body Signals. Grow in Emotional Intelligence. Discover an Embodied Spirituality.* (Beaumont, 2019), 43.

2. Terra A. Mattson, *Courageous: Being Daughters Rooted in Grace* (Colorado Springs, CO: David C Cook, 2020), 160.

3. Jay Stringer, *Unwanted: How Sexual Brokenness Reveals Our Way to Healing* (Colorado Springs, CO: NavPress, 2018).

4. Gene Edwards, *A Tale of Three Kings: A Study in Brokenness* (Wheaton, IL: Tyndale, 1992), 13.

5. Curt Thompson, *Anatomy of the Soul: Surprising Connections between Neuroscience and Spiritual Practices That Can Transform Your Life and Relationships* (Carol Stream, IL: Tyndale, 2010), 23.

6. Ruth Haley Barton, *Sacred Rhythms: Arranging Our Lives for Spiritual Transformation* (Downers Grove, IL: InterVarsity, 2006), 105.

CHAPTER 5: ESCAPISM AND COMPARTMENTALIZATION

1. Lexico.com, s.v. "compartmentalization," www.lexico.com/en/definition /compartmentalization.

2. "The Big Number: Millennials to Overtake Boomers in 2019 as Largest US Population Group," *Washington Post*, January 27, 2019, www.washingtonpost .com/national/health-science/the-big-number-millennials-to-overtake-boomers -in-2019-as-largest-us-population-group/2019/01/25/a566e636-1f4f-11e9-8e21 -59a09ff1e2a1_story.html?utm_term=.6c8d38b24a81.

3. Tyler Schmall, "Americans Spend Half Their Lives in Front of Screens," *New York Post*, August 13, 2018, https://nypost.com/2018/08/13/americans -spend-half-their-lives-in-front-of-screens.

4. Adam Alter, *Irresistible: The Rise of Addictive Technology and the Business of Keeping Us Hooked* (New York: Penguin, 2017), 71–72.

5. Silvana D. Raso, "Gen X vs. Gen Y: Till 'Blank' Do Us Part," *Huffington Post*, November 7, 2011, www.huffpost.com/entry/gen-x-vs-gen-y-till-blank_b_943978.

6. Joel Stein, "Millennials: The Me Me Me Generation," *Time*, May 20, 2013, https://time.com/247/millennials-the-me-me-me-generation; Julia Brailovskaia and Hans-Werner Bierhoff, "The Narcissistic Millennial Generation: A Study of Personality Traits and Online Behavior on Facebook" *Journal of Adult Development* 27, no. 1 (March 2020): 23–35, https://link.springer.com/article/10.1007 /s10804-018-9321-1.

7. *This Is Life with Lisa Ling*, season 5, episode 4, "Screen Addiction," aired October 14, 2018, www.amazon.com/gp/video/detail/B07TRPCJ5S/ref=atv _dp_season_select_s5?tag=tvg_aiv_showcard-20.

8. Celinne Da Costa, "The Millennial Workforce Needs Mentors, Not Managers," *Forbes*, May 25, 2018, www.forbes.com/sites/celinnedacosta/2018/05/25/the -millennial-workforce-needs-mentors-not-managers/#464b7c81127a.

9. Les Parrott, "Toward a More Perfect Union," interview by Carol Pipes, Facts & Trends, January 18, 2016, https://factsandtrends.net/2016/01/18/toward -a-more-perfect-union.

10. Brené Brown, "The Power of Vulnerability" (lecture, TEDxHouston, Houston, TX, June 2010), www.ted.com/talks/brene_brown_the_power_of_vulnerability ?language=en#t-26087.

11. Steven R. Tracy, *Mending the Soul: Understanding and Healing Abuse* (Grand Rapids, MI: Zondervan, 2005), 17.

12. Dorothy S. Hunt, ed., *Love, a Fruit Always in Season: Daily Meditations from the Words of Mother Teresa of Calcutta* (San Francisco: Ignatius, 1987), 129.

CHAPTER 6: NARCISSISM

1. *Diagnostic and Statistical Manual of Mental Disorders*, 5th ed. (Washington, DC: American Psychiatric Association, 2013).

2. If you are familiar with attachment styles, those on the NPD spectrum attract pleasers and victims. See Milan Yerkovich and Kay Yerkovich, *How We Love: Discover Your Love Style, Enhance Your Marriage*, rev. ed. (Colorado Springs, CO: WaterBrook, 2017).

3. R. Glenn Ball and Darrell Puls, *Let Us Prey: The Plague of Narcissist Pastors and What We Can Do about It* (Eugene, OR: Cascade Books, 2017), 111, 114.

4. "The Effects of Gaslighting in Narcissistic Victim Syndrome," Narcissistic Behavior, https://narcissisticbehavior.net/the-effects-of-gaslighting-in-narcissistic -victim-syndrome/.

5. Warren W. Wiersbe, *Be Real: Turning from Hypocrisy to Truth* (Colorado Springs, CO: David C Cook, 2004), 101.

6. Walter Scott, *Marmion: A Tale of Flodden Field* (Baltimore: Joseph Cushing, 1813), 216.

7. Steven R. Tracy, *Mending the Soul: Understanding and Healing Abuse* (Grand Rapids, MI: Zondervan, 2005), 81–83.

8. Tracy, *Mending the Soul*, 83.

9. Barry Sandywell, *Dictionary of Visual Discourse: A Dialectical Lexicon of Terms* (New York: Routledge, 2016), 133.

10. Tracy, *Mending the Soul*, 19.

11. Quoted in Kimi Harris, "Sex Offenders Groom Churches Too," *Christianity Today*, June 8, 2018, www.christianitytoday.com/ct/2018/june-web-only/sex -offenders-groom-churches-too.html.

12. Quoted in Harris, "Sex Offenders."

13. Terra Mattson, quoted in Harris, "Sex Offenders."

14. Tracy, *Mending the Soul*, 39.

15. Tracy, *Mending the Soul*, 96.

16. See Hannah Arendt, *Eichmann in Jerusalem: A Report on the Banality of Evil*, rev. ed. (New York: Penguin, 1965), 21–25. The extreme extent to which Eichmann denied responsibility is seen in his last statement to the court. He declared that his only crime was that he was virtuous, i.e., that he was an obedient, law-abiding German citizen and his virtuous obedience had been abused by Nazi leaders.

17. Tracy, *Mending the Soul*, 39–41.

18. Henry Cloud and John Townsend, *How People Grow: What the Bible Reveals about Personal Growth* (Grand Rapids, MI: Zondervan, 2001), 119.

19. Cloud and Townsend, *How People Grow*, 119.

20. Bill Thrall and Bruce McNicol, Trueface mentoring retreat (Phoenix, AZ), November 4–5, 2019.

21. John M. Gottman, *The Science of Trust: Emotional Attunement for Couples* (New York: Norton, 2011), 46.

22. For more resources on narcissism and health, see Dr. Les Carter at http://drlescarter.com and "Feel Stuck with a Narcissist in Your Life?" at Boundaries, www.boundaries.me/narcissism.

CHAPTER 7: ARROGANCE

1. *Merriam-Webster*, s.v. "arrogance," www.merriam-webster.com/dictionary/arrogance.

2. Candice Millard, *The River of Doubt: Theodore Roosevelt's Darkest Journey* (New York: Doubleday, 2005).

3. Daniel Goleman, *Emotional Intelligence: Why It Can Matter More Than IQ* (New York: Bantam Books, 1997), 13–18.

4. Daniel J. Siegel, *Mindsight: The New Science of Personal Transformation* (New York: Bantam Books, 2010).

5. Daniel Siegel, John and Julie Gottman, Sue Johnson, The Siegel-Gottman Summit, Gottman Institute (Seattle, WA) July 24–25, 2014, www.gottman.com/blog/the-siegel-gottman-summit/.

6. Daniel Siegel, "Parenting for the 21st Century: Building the Neural Circuits for Resilience and Kindness," September 11, 2011, www.youtube.com/watch?v=aV3hp_eaoiE.

CHAPTER 8: BLIND SPOTS

1. Alfred Brendel, quoted in "20 Amazing Quotes from Classical Musicians," www.classicfm.com/discover-music/latest/quotes-classical-musicians/alfred-brendel.

2. Quoted in Andy Serwer, "John Wooden's Best Coaching Tip: Listen," *Fortune*, June 5, 2010, https://archive.fortune.com/2010/06/05/news/newsmakers/john _wooden_obituary_fortune.fortune/index.htm.

3. Wade Luquet, "A Theory of Relationality," introduction to *Imago Relationship Therapy: Perspectives on Theory*, ed. Harville Hendrix et al. (San Francisco: Jossey-Bass, 2005), 6.

4. Diagrams are the intellectual property of Living Wholehearted. Core Values Index is the intellectual property of Taylor Protocols, Inc.

5. Peter F. Drucker, quoted in Oxford Reference, www.oxfordreference.com/view /10.1093/acref/9780191826719.001.0001/q-oro-ed4-00012211.

CHAPTER 9: BURNOUT

1. Dictionary.com, s.v. "efficiency," www.dictionary.com/browse/efficiency?s=t.

2. The Core Values Index Key, Taylor Protocols, Inc., 2007.

3. Ruth Haley Barton, *Strengthening the Soul of Your Leadership: Seeking God in the Crucible of Ministry* (Downers Grove, IL: IVP Books, 2008), 25.

4. Marva J. Dawn and Eugene H. Peterson, *The Unnecessary Pastor: Rediscovering the Call* (Grand Rapids, MI: Eerdmans, 2000), 14.

5. Barton, *Strengthening the Soul*, 26–27.

6. Henry Cloud, *Boundaries for Leaders: Why Some People Get Results and Others Don't* (New York: HarperCollins, 2013), 14.

7. Cloud, *Boundaries for Leaders*, 15.

8. James M. Kouzes and Barry Z. Posner, *Credibility: How Leaders Gain and Lose It, Why People Demand It* (San Francisco: Jossey-Bass, 2003), 249–50.

CHAPTER 10: ISOLATION

1. Bill Thrall, Bruce McNicol, Ken McElrath, *The Ascent of a Leader: How Ordinary Relationships Develop Extraordinary Character and Influence* (San Francisco: Jossey-Bass, 1999), 20.

2. Courageous Girls, www.mycourageousgirls.com.

3. Dietrich Bonhoeffer, *Life Together* (New York: Harper Row, 1958), 10.

4. "1097. Ginóskó," Bible Hub, https://biblehub.com/greek/1097.htm.

5. Harville Hendrix, *Getting the Love You Want: A Guide for Couples*, rev. ed. (New York: Henry Holt, 2019), xix.

CHAPTER 11: SURVIVAL

1. A. H. Maslow, "A Theory of Human Motivation," *Psychological Review* 50, no. 4 (1943), 370–96.

2. Leadership Advance conference, Murdock Charitable Trust (Vancouver, WA), December 5, 2019.

3. Sue C. Bratton et al., *Child Parent Relationship Therapy (CPRT) Treatment Manual: A 10-Session Filial Therapy Model for Training Parents* (New York: Routledge, 2006), xix.

4. Milan Yerkovich and Kay Yerkovich, *How We Love: Discover Your Love Style, Enhance Your Marriage*, rev. ed. (Colorado Springs, CO: WaterBrook, 2017), 13–17.

5. Curt Thompson, *Anatomy of the Soul: Surprising Connections between Neuroscience and Spiritual Practices That Can Transform Your Life and Relationships* (Carol Stream, IL: Tyndale, 2010), 42.

6. Adapted from Terra A. Mattson, *Courageous: Being Daughters Rooted in Grace* (Colorado Springs, CO: David C Cook, 2020), 77.

CHAPTER 12: HIDING

1. Henry Cloud, *Necessary Endings: The Employees, Businesses, and Relationships That All of Us Have to Give Up in Order to Move Forward* (New York: HarperCollins, 2010), 122.

2. Terra A. Mattson, *Courageous: Being Daughters Rooted in Grace* (Colorado Springs, CO: David C Cook, 2020), 157–59.

3. Cloud, *Necessary Endings*, 144–45.

4. Tom Rath and Barry Conchie, *Strengths Based Leadership: Great Leaders, Teams, and Why People Follow* (New York: Gallup, 2008), 78.

5. Aaron Lucchetti and Tom Lauricella, "Investors Were Told They Had a Total of $64.8 Billion," *Wall Street Journal*, March 11, 2009, www.wsj.com/articles /SB123673521911590783; Grant McCool and Martha Graybow, "Madoff Faces Life in Prison on 11 Criminal Charges," Reuters, March 11, 2009, www.reuters .com/article/us-madoff/madoff-faces-life-in-prison-on-11-criminal-charges -idUSN1046349920090311; Jonathan Stempel, "Bernard Madoff Wants to Make 'Dying, Personal Plea' for Freedom," Reuters, March 12, 2020, www.reuters .com/article/us-usa-crime-madoff/bernard-madoff-wants-to-make-dying-personal -plea-for-freedom-idUSKBN20Z27J; John F. Wasik, "Inside the Mind of Madoff: When Did Scam Really Begin?," *Forbes*, October 3, 2012, www.forbes.com/sites /johnwasik/2012/10/03/inside-the-mind-of-madoff-when-did-scam-really-begin /#eebb6884ec83; David Teather, "Bernard Madoff Receives Maximum 150 Year Sentence," *Guardian*, June 30, 2009, www.theguardian.com/business/2009/jun /29/bernard-madoff-sentence.

6. Diana B. Henriques, "Andrew Madoff, Who Told of His Father's Swindle, Dies at 48," *New York Times*, September 3, 2014, www.nytimes.com/2014/09/04 /business/andrew-madoff-son-of-convicted-financier-dies-at-48.html; Complaint, SEC v. Madoff, 08 Civ. 10791, December 11, 2008, 5–6, www.sec.gov/litigation /complaints/2008/comp-madoff121108.pdf.

7. Bernard L. Madoff, "Bernard L. Madoff's Statement to the Court," *New York Times*, June 29, 2009, www.nytimes.com/2009/06/30/business/30bernietext.html.

8. Thomas Zambito, Jose Martinez, and Corky Siemaszko, "Bye, Bye, Bernie: Ponzi King Madoff Sentenced to 150 Years," *Daily News*, June 29, 2009, www.nydailynews.com/news/money/bye-bye-bernie-ponzi-king-madoff -sentenced-150-years-article-1.373445; Robert Frank and Amir Efrati, "'Evil' Madoff Gets 150 Years in Epic Fraud," *Wall Street Journal*, June 30, 2009, www.wsj.com/articles/SB124604151653862301; Sentence, United States v. Madoff, 09 CR 213 (DC), June 29, 2009, 43, 47, www.justice.gov/usao-sdny /file/762821/download.

9. Scott Cohn, "In New Emails, Madoff Says Fraud Wasn't So Bad," CNBC, April 7, 2015, www.cnbc.com/2015/04/07/in-new-emails-madoff-says-fraud -wasnt-so-bad.html.

10. "Monica Lewinsky Scandal," last modified June 10, 2019, History.com, www.history.com/topics/1990s/monica-lewinsky.

11. Bill Clinton, speech, Washington, DC (August 17, 1998), *Washington Post*, www.washingtonpost.com/wp-srv/politics/special/clinton/stories/text081898.htm.

12. Ruth Haley Barton, *Strengthening the Soul of Your Leadership: Seeking God in the Crucible of Ministry* (Downers Grove, IL: IVP Books, 2008), 48.

13. Barton, *Strengthening the Soul*, 49.

14. Kenya Evelyn, "Bill Clinton Says Monica Lewinsky Affair Was to 'Manage Anxiety,'" *Guardian*, March 6, 2020, www.theguardian.com/us-news/2020/mar/06/bill-clinton-monica-lewinsky-affair-anxiety.

15. John Lynch, Bruce McNicol, and Bill Thrall, *The Cure: What If God Isn't Who You Think He Is and Neither Are You?*, (Phoenix, AZ: Trueface Ministries, 2010).

16. Joseph M. Stowell, *Redefining Leadership: Character-Driven Habits of Effective Leaders* (Grand Rapids, MI: Zondervan, 2014), 143.

CONCLUSION: HOPE FOR WHOLEHEARTED LEADERSHIP

1. Romney M. Moseley, *Becoming a Self before God: Critical Transformations* (Nashville, TN: Abingdon, 1991), 41.

2. D. L. Moody, "The Seven 'Walks' of Ephesians," in *Short Talks* (Chicago: Moody, 1900), 38.

3. Robert K. Greenleaf, *Servant Leadership: A Journey into the Nature of Legitimate Power and Greatness* (Mahwah, NJ: Paulist Press, 1977), 357.

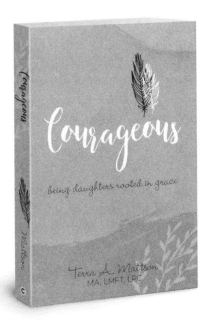

Courageous Women Know They Can't Do It Alone

Becoming and raising daughters who have a real relationship with a loving, grace-filled God is difficult in a rapidly changing culture. In this highly practical book, the founder of the Courageous Girls movement draws on her decades of experience to nurture women, along with their daughters, toward a journey of becoming women of courage.

Learn more! Follow Terra at @terramattson on Instagram.

Available in print and digital editions wherever books are sold.

Join the Movement of Becoming a Wholehearted Leader

Whether leading in the home, work, or community, Jeff & Terra are tackling relevant issues that every leader faces. Subscribe to their weekly podcasts to continue shrinking your integrity gap and to stay connected to the resources coming out of *Living Wholehearted*.

Subscribe to the Living Wholehearted Podcast Today!

www.livingwholehearted.com